Haunted Portland

Haunted Portland

From Pirates to Ghost Brides

Roxie J. Zwicker

Haunted
America

Published by Haunted America
A Division of The History Press
Charleston, SC 29403
www.historypress.net

Cover design by Marshall Hudson.
All images courtesy of the author.

First published 2007

Manufactured in the United States

ISBN 978.1.59629.282.6

Library of Congress Cataloging-in-Publication Data

Zwicker, Roxie J.
Haunted Portland : from pirates to ghost brides / Roxie J. Zwicker.
p. cm.
Includes bibliographical references.
ISBN-13: 978-1-59629-282-6 (alk. paper)
1. Ghosts--Maine--Portland. 2. Haunted places--Maine--Portland. I. Title.
BF1472.U6Z945 2007
133.109741'91--dc22
2007029683

To those who truly believed in me.
And to those who believe.

Contents

Introduction

Does this book have you wondering about the haunted past of one of Maine's most fascinating cities? It seems as though in this old city, ghost stories are told in a whisper, if they are told at all. It has been quite a challenge to unearth these tales to share with you. While there are ghostly tales about Portland, they have been hiding in old newspaper articles and lingering in dusty archives. Visiting these places and asking questions has certainly helped to set the scene, yet I left with even more questions. Why does it seem that many people are hesitant to talk about ghosts or haunted places? Could it be an old Yankee attitude that ghosts are nothing more than folklore, and a practical person wouldn't and shouldn't discuss the paranormal? Is the haunted history dark and evil? Why should we dredge up stories of spirits in this modern and scientific world? Could the acceptance of a belief in the paranormal bring about other questions, ones that we may be afraid to answer? Certainly some stories have dark moments, where mysterious shadows may overtake the light of our day-to-day world.

The beginnings of New England folklore arrived with the first settlers, and many tales carried through the Native American culture. There are numerous books from the eighteenth and nineteenth centuries that have New England folktales; all one has to do is to take a look. Samuel Adams Drake, William Root Bliss and Nathaniel Hawthorne are just a few of New England's early writers, assembling true tales, tall tales and mysteries of the Northeastern states.

A quote by Nathaniel Hawthorne states it simply: "Blessed are all simple emotion, be they dark or bright." Thinking about that statement

The city of Portland blends the past with the present.

certainly makes one think. We cannot have light without dark; could we also say we cannot have a house with a compelling history that does not yield a few shadowy ghost stories? With some of the oldest settlements in the country and the tragedies that were a part of each, there is some latent impression that has remained over the years. Ghost stories can also be another way to view and understand a location's history and legacy.

We didn't always have television or the movies to entertain us. In the early days of our nation our entertainment was stories that were passed down to us from others in our small but growing communities. Some storytellers went from town to town telling their tales, and in many cases picking up more tales along the way. Added to their collection were the stories of the spirit world, which go back thousands of years and are found in every culture on the planet. The stories created superstitions and legends that weaved their ways into the history books. From ancient literature to historic customs, mysterious history is all around us in New England. Are we so set in our modern ways that we cannot accept the possibilities of what we may not know? These tales all have ties to the past. Be it a historic location, person or event, these are the tales that grew up around them, and the stories continue to grow and evolve as time goes on.

A poll by the Gallup organization in 2005 revealed that nearly 75 percent of Americans believe in paranormal activity in some form, including ESP (41 percent believed), haunted houses (37 percent), ghosts (32 percent) and communication with the dead (21 percent). With that being said, I invite those of you who are skeptical, those who love a good ghost story around the campfire and some of you who may have always wondered about that house down the street to step into the haunted past of Portland, Maine. Through these pages, I promise you will not look at some of these locations the same again.

To set the scene, let us examine the history of this fascinating city. Portland accounts for one quarter of Maine's total population and is the largest city in Maine. Portland was originally known as Machigonne, which meant "great neck" in the local Native American language. The first official settler in the Portland area was Walter Bagnall, who in 1628 set up a trading post on Richmond's Island. Unfortunately, he was murdered in 1631 because he cheated the Indians with whom he had traded. In 1632, when English settlers arrived to establish a fishing and trading settlement, the name was changed to Casco. The first dwelling was built on what is now the corner of Hancock and Fore Streets. In

1658, the name of the settlement was changed to Falmouth by the Massachusetts commissioners, as the state of Maine had not yet achieved statehood. In 1675, the city of Falmouth was completely destroyed by the Wampanoag tribe and their allies during King Philip's War (King Philip was the English name given to the chief of the Wampanoag). King Philip felt his people had been wronged by the colonists, and he led a brutal campaign against the settlers. In 1676, all of the thirty-four colonists in Falmouth were either captured or brutally killed. The Indians set the new colony ablaze and burned the small village to the ground, leaving nothing but a charred landscape.

In 1678 the settlement was rebuilt, but continued conflict between settlers and natives led to the city's destruction a second time in 1690. The Indians ambushed thirty men who were suspicious of the Indians' activity on Munjoy Hill. Fourteen men from the party of colonists were killed, while the others escaped to the newly built garrison house. Later that night under the cover of darkness, the white men fled to Fort Loyall. Once again the homes and structures of the new settlement were reduced to ashes by a rampant fire set by the Indians. While at the fort, the townspeople were under siege by both the Indians and the French. The French promised the surrounded townspeople an opportunity to leave the fort and told them that they could leave unharmed. However, the French went back on their word, and as soon as the gates to the fort opened, the townspeople didn't have the slightest chance. The Indians were given free reign to murder and scalp the settlers, and they did so with a bloodlust the village had not yet seen. There was not a sole survivor, and for two years the bodies were left where they were slain, as the dark shadow of the village remained quiet and uninhabited.

Although peace was declared in 1699, it took some time for people to come back and rebuild the settlement. By 1718, twenty families had moved into the area. Finally the village had a chance to grow without the risk of attack. The winters were brutal and disease, such as the throat distemper, made life difficult. However, the community grew and prospered through maritime trade and lumbering, as the area offered large trees that could serve as masts and large planks. Thereafter the early beginnings of shipbuilding helped Falmouth prosper and thrive.

During the Revolution in 1775, Falmouth suffered under the Stamp Act imposed by Britain, and the inhabitants rebelled. In general, citizens of Falmouth sympathized with the Boston Patriots, and they rejoiced about the Boston Tea Party. Falmouth sent good men to join the

Revolutionary side at the Battle of Lexington and Concord. A clash over a ship captained by Thomas Coulson, a British Loyalist, added to the fervor of the times. The captain wanted to send a load of masts to Britain; however, the Patriots would not allow it, and they hid the masts up along the Fore River. Meanwhile, a group of rowdy Patriots captured Captain Henry Mowatt, who commanded a British sloop of war. His capture was unfortunately brief, and he soon plotted revenge.

Captain Mowatt knew of the situation with the masts and how rebellious the community was growing. He arrived in Falmouth with four armed British vessels and terms. The orders came swiftly and required the townspeople to turn over all of their munitions, from cannons to small arms. Not ready to give in, the townspeople rejected the captain's terms, and he levied his punishment. He ordered the vessels to fire upon the town for twelve hours straight. Over one hundred British soldiers stormed the city, burning everything to the ground. Most of Falmouth was destroyed, leaving only one hundred out of five hundred buildings standing. Many residents moved away, never to return after the incident, while others stood resolute in their opposition to the British, as this devastation created an atmosphere of steadfastness for the Revolution, with no turning back.

The following perspective on the devastating fire was written in the *New England Gazette* on November 23, 1775.

> *The savage and brutal barbarity of our enemies in burning Falmouth, is a full demonstration that there is not the least remains of virtue, wisdom or humanity in the British court and that they are fully determined with fire and sword, to butcher and destroy, beggar and enslave the whole American people. Therefore we expect soon to break off all kinds of connection with Britain and form into a Grand Republic of the American Colonies, which will, by the blessing of heaven, soon work out our salvation and perpetuate the liberties, increase the wealth, the power and the glory of the western world.*

In 1786, as a newly independent nation grew, so did the city now renamed Portland. Prosperity shined down on the city once again. Portland quickly prospered and rebuilt, shipping increased and the building of Portland Head Lighthouse further established that this was an important port on the Atlantic Coast. In 1807, the Portland Observatory was built on Munjoy Hill, which was important to maritime trade as it provided a lookout for ships in distress. The wives of ship captains and sailors could climb the tower and watch for their loved ones' arrivals in Portland.

In 1820, Maine declared its statehood and separated from Massachusetts. Portland was the first capital until 1832. Just twenty years later, in 1852, Portland boasted over a dozen shipyards in operation. In 1851, prominent Portland resident Neal Dow led the temperance movement, believing that drinking and drunkenness were evil and that the temptation needed to be destroyed. The Maine Legislature passed the first prohibition law, which forbade the manufacture and sale of liquor. This came nearly seventy years before the national Prohibition Act was enacted in 1920.

On Independence Day, 1866, Portland was preparing a Fourth of July celebration. With the recent end to the Civil War, the city was ready for joyous festivities. The joy quickly turned to tragedy as the nation saw its worst tragedy of the time take place in Portland. No one is exactly sure how the fire started; some say it began with a firecracker being tossed into a boatyard on Commercial Street. Quickly the flames spread to a lumberyard and then to Brown's Sugarhouse on Maple Street. Winds drove the fire throughout the city, and the fire raged and consumed everything in its path. Despite efforts, the uncontrollable fire swept through historic homes, public buildings, warehouses and tenement houses. The view from the Eastern Cemetery on the hill revealed the incredible destruction. In the end, 1,800 buildings were destroyed and 10,000 people were homeless when the fire finally burned itself out.

Tent cities popped up all over Portland, and rebuilding commenced. Bricks were salvaged from the fires and were used to begin the reconstruction efforts. These disasters and the subsequent rebuilding led the city to adopt the phoenix as its symbol and "Resurgam" as its motto—meaning, "I Shall Rise Again." The legend of the phoenix has roots in ancient Egyptian mythology, as this ancient bird became the symbol of the ability to rise out of and above decay, ruin and destruction. Portland once again emerged a beautiful, industrious and proud city. The structures that were built as the city resurfaced were elegant Victorian buildings and homes, most of which still exist today and add to the character of Portland.

In 1918, the city of Portland was subjected to the dreaded Spanish flu epidemic. Across the city homes displayed black wreaths on their doors in memory of loved ones who had passed away from this mysterious disease. It was said that about 28 percent of the nation's population suffered, and 500,000 to 675,000 died. The state of Maine totaled nearly 4,000 dead

Portland Harbor is quite busy. In this image one of the working tugboats passes Spring Point Ledge Lighthouse.

by the end of 1918. The flu attacked with a severe fever and pneumonia. People without symptoms could be struck suddenly and within hours be too feeble to walk; many died the next day. Symptoms included a blue tint to the face and coughing up blood caused by severe obstruction of the lungs. Throughout Portland there were daily funeral carriages that carried the dead to their final resting places. It was thought that the flu originated in Europe and was brought back by soldiers to Fort Devens, and from there it quickly spread. The city of Portland closed schools, churches, movie houses and dance halls to stop the transmission of the fatal ailment. By January 1919, the Spanish flu epidemic began to draw to a close, and eventually it did not return.

Times in the twentieth century gave Portland years of prosperity, especially during World War II when government contracts afforded everyone opportunity. There were some dark days, when the city turned into a gritty seaport and once-bustling waterfront businesses were abandoned as the beauty of the city became overshadowed. However, through the later years of the twentieth century, the city transformed, culturally and historically. Portland offers much these days—a thriving retail district, a modern business center and a haven for artists. A deep appreciation and movement for the preservation of Portland's historic buildings and homes surfaced over the years as well.

The incredible history of this city that has been burned to the ground three times creates a compelling scene for spirited stories. Facing adversity time and time again, the city has always managed to come back stronger than before. Perhaps Portland came back with some ghosts of the past as well.

Ghostly Specters of the
William E. Gould House

A lightning rod with a mystical eye looks over the William E. Gould House on State Street in Portland. This gorgeous brick home was built in 1884, and its castle-like edifice beckons passersby to take a closer look. The noticeably tall chimneys of the home add to the distinctive style of architecture. But even the most beautiful homes have ghosts

The William E. Gould House is rumored to have several spirits.

hiding in their closets—or basements. The William E. Gould House has since been converted into luxurious apartments, and over the years many of the residents have claimed that the house is a haven for spirits and unexplained activity.

Phantom footfalls have been heard in the basement, and a mysterious presence seems to shadow those who venture down there at night. A presence has been known to brush past people passing through the hallways as they make their way back to their apartments. One resident claimed to feel a tapping on her shoulder as if someone was trying to get her attention; however, she was surprised when the mysterious feeling offered no source, as she was all alone.

The home was converted into a doctor's office for a number of years, and some people attribute the spirits to the days when patients visited the house. The doctor, who was nicknamed Dr. Death, was thought to be a man who used unusual treatments on some of his patients. Some believe that the spirits are the doctor's patients who continually return looking for him. There is even the rumor that the house was built over an old Native American burial ground and perhaps that is the cause for the high number of spirited encounters in the home.

The Western Cemetery

Located on the Western Promenade of the Portland peninsula is the Western Cemetery, the city's second official burying ground. Originally established in 1829 on a sloping hill, this site is the final resting place for many of Portland's prominent and prosperous citizens of the past. Buried here are such distinguished residents as Portland's greatest capitalist, John Bundy Brown, and the family of Henry Wadsworth Longfellow. The Western Cemetery is in one of the most affluent areas in Portland; the streets are lined with grand mansions and elegant homes built from the Victorian era to the early twentieth century. During the cemetery's early days, many families had their relatives' remains moved here from smaller plots throughout the city.

Given the cemetery's apparently favorable location, it is surprising to discover the extensive vandalism here. On a visit during a dreary spring afternoon, I was greeted by a row of broken tombstones, the top halves leaning awkwardly this way and that. There are winding pathways that lead between rows of pitch pine and family plots where the grass grows high, as if to camouflage the few small stones that somehow have survived unbroken. From July 1988 to August 1989, 1,943 gravestones were vandalized and destroyed in Portland's cemeteries, with approximately 1,000 in the Western Cemetery alone. The blatant desecration is visible throughout the grounds, with more stones broken and shattered than are standing. It is quite amazing to see that unappreciative people with baseball bats can destroy history and someone's memory with just one swing. The perpetrators were eventually caught, but no matter the punishment they received, the

The Western Cemetery is also home to the Longfellow family tomb.

damage is irreversible and still quite visible. It is no wonder, then, that there are stories of unrest in this seemingly peaceful resting place.

From the entrance to the graveyard along the walking path to the right, there is a wall of tombs. One of the most noticeable names is Longfellow. This granite tomb was built into the hillside behind beautiful mansions. Just slightly weathered, the tomb appears to be in good condition. Bordering the edges of the tomb and across the top grow wildflowers of every color. Their aroma is quite fragrant in the air. While you stand in front of the tomb, you might be surprised to learn that the decedents have gone missing. The placement of the Longfellow family remains is quite a mystery, as the tomb was rumored to be vacant.

One of the most widely read American poets, Henry Wadsworth Longfellow was born in Portland, Maine, and he often returned for frequent visits. Although he is buried in the famous Mount Auburn Cemetery in Cambridge, Massachusetts, according to records his parents, two brothers and other relatives were laid to rest in this tomb here in the Western Cemetery.

During restoration work in 1986, it was written in a *Portland Press Herald* newspaper article that the tomb was discovered to be completely empty. This surprising revelation had been made while workers were replacing the bricks that sealed the tomb entrance closed. Some speculated that the bodies had been moved to the Evergreen Cemetery in Portland, yet there are no records available to confirm that. Further research stated that the remains were not moved to Duxbury, Massachusetts, where the family also had ties. So where are the bodies?

One theory is that the remains are hidden behind a secret wall in the tomb, although there has been no definite proof of this. The reasoning behind that thought is that perhaps Anne Longfellow Pierce (who was the last occupant of the Longfellow House on Congress Street) had reason to believe the tomb would be vandalized, and therefore safeguarded the bodies behind an inner wall of the tomb. Well, whatever truth there is behind this unusual circumstance remains unknown; but what is known is that by all accounts the tomb appears to be completely empty.

Making your way down the winding paths, you will find a large Irish American section of the burial ground for some of the immigrants who came to Portland during the late nineteenth and early twentieth centuries. There is even a monument that memorializes those who died in the Great Potato Famine of 1845–49. The sturdy stones that still remain in this area have wonderful Celtic designs and carvings.

An investigative paranormal group based in Maine decided to do some ghostly research in the cemetery, and they discovered that there was something unusual going on here. Members of the group attempted to capture what are commonly referred to as EVPs. EVP, or electronic voice phenomenon, is the alleged communication by spirits through tape recorders and other electronic devices. EVP basically concerns unexpected voices found in recording media. Many people believe that it is a form of after-death communication. Typically, a voice recorder is engaged and the person performing the reading asks short questions, hoping for a response from the spirit world. Most responses are rather short and are usually missed until playback.

The results of the Maine investigative group's EVP recordings revealed that while members of the group appeared to be the only people in attendance, there was also a spirited presence at the Western Cemetery. The playback of their recordings led to the discovery of a conversation moving around them after they asked questions such as, "Who else is here?" The voices that came through sounded like a discussion between a group of people getting louder and louder, as though these people (or spirits) moved close to the microphone on the recorder and then moved away. The words of the conversation could not be identified, as there were so many people speaking over one another. But the strangest thing was how the recording got louder and then softer, as if these unseen spirits were coming forward in waves. It was relayed that the sounds were very similar to those in a restaurant with several people talking around you, when it is difficult to discern what each person is saying. The group concluded that there was no other plausible source for the mysterious voices, as there was no one else around. Perhaps something or someone from beyond the grave was responsible.

Many people believe in using EVP to capture messages from the dearly departed. In the case of the Western Cemetery, there appear to be several messages that the spirits there want to share with the curious.

The Eastern Cemetery

One of the oldest burial grounds in Maine, the Eastern Cemetery was officially established in 1668; however, it is said that interments began earlier than that. George Cleeve, one of the original settlers, who is often referred to as the father of Portland, designated this land to be a burial ground. When he passed away in 1666, he was buried just behind his home, which was customary at the time. Soon thereafter, the cemetery around him was officially established. Unfortunately, it is said that Cleeve's remains were uprooted just two hundred years later, after Portland's Great Fire of 1866. As the reconstruction of local sites began, a retaining wall was built along Federal Street. In doing so, part of the hillside of the burial ground was dug out, along with Cleeve's remains. The earth (and what resided in it) was removed and was said to have been brought over to Back Cove and deposited, basically being used as fill.

In the nineteenth century, this six-acre burial ground was referred to as the "field of ancient graves." Originally surrounded by a mossy stone wall, the cemetery once boasted an enormously tall Norway pine tree that was so large it could be seen in the distance by those entering Portland Harbor. Some of the first people buried here were victims of Indian attacks, including the twelve men who were killed on September 21, 1689, near the Deering mansion, and another thirteen men who were killed by a party of Indians in an ambush close to the cemetery just a few years later.

In the cemetery you will find the memorial to Colonel William Tyng, who received his commission from British General Gage in Boston in 1774. He later fled to New York and Nova Scotia but returned to Maine in 1793 and settled in nearby Gorham, where he passed away in 1807.

There are thousands of graves in the seventeenth-century Eastern Cemetery.

This ten-foot-high monument of red freestone and marble panels was commissioned by his wife.

Other graves include those of Captain Jacob Adams and his wife, along with two others who drowned while onboard the schooner *Charles* (see the chapter on the ghost bride Lydia Carver), which wrecked on Richmond Island on Cape Elizabeth. You will also find the grave of Daniel Manly, who holds the distinction of being Portland's first bank robber in 1818. Two men, Thomas Bird and Solomon Goodwin, are also buried here; they each were hanged for murder in the late eighteenth century.

There are approximately seventy-five underground tombs in the cemetery as well, although it has been said that they have collapsed over the years from the shifting of the ground caused by burials and visitors. According to cemetery records, the cemetery is the final resting place for more than four thousand of the city's earliest residents. Space for burials became quite cramped, so many remains were buried inordinately close to one another and at unusual angles, according to records.

A plaque stands just outside the cemetery that informs visitors that the burial ground is the final resting place for many abolitionists.

People who provided safe houses as part of the Underground Railroad, campaigned against slavery and assisted African Americans to freedom are remembered here.

Many of those buried here are easily linked to the sea with a review of the epitaphs. One stone reads, "Lost at Sea," while another reads, "Executed for murder on the high seas," and still another reads, "Killed by a fall from masthead." The following is a very poignant and moving epitaph from one of the stones in this old burial ground.

> *In memory of Mrs. Mary Stonehouse of Boston relict of the late Capt. Robert Stonehouse, she was drowned from the Portland Packet. July 12 1807. Aged 62 years. From the cold bosom of the wave, Where others found a watr'y grave, This lifeless corpse was borne, and here The friends of virtue drop the tear That mourn the much lamented dead, But oh! What bitter tears are shed For fathers, mothers, babes who sleep In the dark mansions of the deep. Then young & old, rich & poor prepare For God may summons when you'r not aware.*

Most of the old trees have since been cut down or have succumbed to the elements over time. Today you will find young trees planted throughout the cemetery, ready to take root and provide shade to the multitude of gravestones that still stand. There are no stones that remain from the seventeenth century, and the oldest remaining stone dates from May 23, 1717. Walking to the farthest edges of the burial ground yields views of some of the most striking carvings, including winged skulls (soul effigies) and skulls and crossbones. There are numerous broken stones that act more like tripping hazards than memorials hidden in the tall, swaying grass. So once you stray off of the path, it is best to be wise of what lies underfoot.

There are numerous unmarked graves throughout the cemetery. Located in the southwest corner of the grounds was an area for Quaker burials. There are also two unmarked sections that served as African American burial grounds. Another section, called the "Strangers" section, was set aside for the poor and unknown; this section is also unmarked. Oddly enough, the city of Portland allowed for the burial of two bodies per grave in the "Strangers" area.

Near the Congress Street entrance stands a small Gothic Revival cottage, under which was the city tomb that was used during the winter months. It was reported that in 1868 there were 111 bodies awaiting burial

An example of one of the tombstones dating from 1775 has a skull and crossbones motif.

in the spring, when the ground thawed. Today this attractive building is used as a storage shed for the cemetery. Also along the Congress Street entrance is a beautiful black iron fence and gate, which were salvaged some years ago from renovations at the Portland High School. The fence adds to the Gothic charm of the entrance to the burial ground.

Interments ended in 1858, when the ancient boneyard was filled to capacity. Just next door to the cemetery is the North School, which was built in 1867 but was renovated in the 1980s as senior citizen housing. In 1973, the cemetery was placed on the National Register of Historic Places. The cemetery gates are typically locked at all times, except for the occasional special event. The city is striving to keep out vagrants and vandals; therefore, most visitors are forced to peer through the fence to get a good view of the grounds. A shop across the street from the cemetery entrance keeps a key to the gates for hopeful visitors.

It is said that while peering through the fence, you might see some of the ancient ghostly spirits of the Eastern Cemetery. According to local legend, a midnight discussion is carried on in the burial ground by two sworn and bitter enemies. The spirits are said to be those of Captain Samuel Blyth, commander of the British warship the *Boxer*, and Lieutenant William Burrows, commander of the American *Enterprise* during the War of 1812. The intense battle took place just north of Casco Bay, off Monhegan Island, and sadly resulted in the death of both men. The *Enterprise* was victorious and brought the captured British ship into Portland. Side by side, the two men were buried in the Eastern Cemetery, both with full military honors.

The apparitions of each are said to appear by their gravesides engaged in a loud shouting match, perhaps still engaged in a war of words. Those who have witnessed the confrontation claim that as soon as the spirits notice they are being watched by someone, they disappear behind the gravestones, leaving no trace except for a fine mist. So if you hear sounds late at night coming from within the locked gates of the Eastern Cemetery and you find a light mist in the air, perhaps it is two of the many spirits of the ancient boneyard.

The Gargoyle House

M erriam Webster defines a gargoyle as the following: "*noun* Origins: 13th Century. 1a: a spout in the form of a grotesque human or animal figure projecting from a roof gutter to throw rainwater clear of a building b: a grotesquely carved figure." There are many superstitions associated with gargoyles, including that they are guardians that can ward off unwanted spirits and other creatures. Some folklore even suggests that they come alive at night when everyone is asleep, so that they can offer protection during the vulnerable hours. Some gargoyles were designed with wings so that they could fly over villages and keep watch over greater distances. At dawn, the gargoyles are said to return to their roosts until the next sunset.

One of the most impressive collections of limestone demons and stone gargoyles is at the Washington National Cathedral in Washington, D.C., but if don't feel like traveling that far all you need to do is find your way to Portland. The architecture throughout Portland offers much to those with a keen eye for detail. There are numerous buildings with accents ranging from carved seashells, faces, scrollwork, flora and fauna, as well as gargoyles. Portland boasts several buildings with gargoyles, such as the ones on the entrance to the Oxford building (built 1886–87) located on Middle Street, designed by renowned architect John Calvin Stevens I. One street in a city neighborhood offers a most unusual collection. Located on Coyle Street is a beautiful duplex that was built in 1893. This gray and green house with yellow trim and neatly manicured front garden appears to be quite inviting. If you take a closer look at the house, you'll notice something odd, however: there are small stonework creatures that seem to be peering out at you from the peaks, doorways and chimney of the house.

The fascinating Gargoyle House.

Climbing across one of the exterior walls is a large, yellow gargoyle with a sneering expression. Mounted atop the chimney there is a large, winged gargoyle ready to take flight and circle the neighborhood. Be sure to look at the other chimneys for other dark guardians. There are fantastic dragons peering down from the upper areas of the house. Over the doorways there are gargoyles that seem to be following every move you make as you walk around the house. There are so many gargoyles that you might be surprised to notice one that you may have missed at first glance. Was it there the first time you looked, or did it just appear?

The owner of the house decided that the house needed protection when he purchased it in the 1990s. He had lost two homes to the bank and was looking for a little extra protection from evil spirits. These evil spirits he described might be lawyers and bankers. The house had stood vacant for a number of years, but it seemed to come back to life when the new owner purchased it, as he also completed renovations to the exterior. The final touches were adding the gargoyles.

When the installation of the gargoyles was complete, the house became a destination for the curious. People would drive by the house to get a look at this most unusual display of creatures. Neighborhood children would bring their friends over to stand on the sidewalk and marvel at the guardians of the house. Well, call it good fortune; it's now been more than ten years since the first gargoyle took its roost, and the house is doing well under the same ownership. Perhaps one night as you are walking down the street in Portland you may see a shadow pass over the moon. It may not be a cloud, but instead one of the gargoyles keeping a watch on the Coyle Street house.

Portland Head Lighthouse

One of the most photographed lighthouses in the United States is the Portland Head Lighthouse. This gorgeous lighthouse has appeared in hundreds of advertisements and photographs as the quintessential New England lighthouse. Perched on a rocky cliff at the entrance to Portland Harbor, the lighthouse offers views that are nothing short of spectacular. The building attracts hundreds of thousands of visitors every year, and on any given weekend throughout the year you can see wedding parties being photographed on the grounds of the lighthouse.

From this vantage point, you can get a wonderful view of the many Casco Bay Islands and several other lighthouses, such as Ram Island Ledge light and the twin lights of Cape Elizabeth. The maritime traffic is quite busy through the harbor with cargo ships, local ferries and the occasional cruise liner, such as the prestigious *Queen Mary II* and the Celebrity Cruises liner the *Constellation*, one of the largest cruise liners in the world. In addition, the seafaring traffic related to the very significant fishing industry affords visitors views of the lobster boats and fishing trawlers that travel throughout the bay.

The first lighthouse in Maine, Portland Head Light, was constructed in 1791 and stood at seventy-two feet tall. The lighthouse was so important that the first lighthouse keeper was appointed by George Washington. After just four years of being keeper, Captain Joseph Greenleaf died of a stroke in his boat in the Fore River. The main house was in poor condition for many years, and there was even a point when the foundation was being undermined by rats.

In 1869, a strong hurricane knocked the lighthouse's fog bell into a chasm, almost killing lighthouse Keeper Joshua Strout. Joshua was a

Do the spirits of lighthouse keepers past still haunt Portland Head Lighthouse?

popular lighthouse keeper, known for his friendly disposition and his parrot, Billy. Billy the parrot would alert the keeper when bad weather approached, and the bird had a very colorful vocabulary.

On Christmas Eve, 1886, the lighthouse keepers were surprised during Christmas dinner. The British barque *Annie C. Maguire* ran aground along the sweeping ledge next to the lighthouse. The lighthouse keeper rescued the entire crew, including the captain, his wife and their twelve-year-old son. There was enough food on hand to maintain the crew for three days at Portland Head Lighthouse. Today, visitors to the lighthouse can view the hand-painted memorial on the rocks where the wreck occurred over one hundred years ago.

It is said that Portland Head Lighthouse inspired Henry Wadsworth Longfellow to pen the poem "The Lighthouse."

The rocky ledge runs far into the sea,
and on its outer point, some miles away,
the Lighthouse lifts its massive masonry,
A pillar of fire by night, of cloud by day.

Even at this distance I can see the tides,
Upheaving, break unheard along its base,
A speechless wrath, that rises and subsides
in the white tip and tremor of the face.

And as the evening darkens, lo! how bright,
through the deep purple of the twilight air,
Beams forth the sudden radiance of its light,
with strange, unearthly splendor in the glare!

Not one alone; from each projecting cape
And perilous reef along the ocean's verge,
Starts into life a dim, gigantic shape,
Holding its lantern o'er the restless surge.

Like the great giant Christopher it stands
Upon the brink of the tempestuous wave,
Wading far out among the rocks and sands,
The night-o'er taken mariner to save.

And the great ships sail outward and return
Bending and bowing o'er the billowy swells,
And ever joyful, as they see it burn
They wave their silent welcome and farewells.

From Pirates to Ghost Brides

They come forth from the darkness, and their sails
Gleam for a moment only in the blaze,
And eager faces, as the light unveils
Gaze at the tower, and vanish while they gaze.

The mariner remembers when a child,
on his first voyage, he saw it fade and sink;
And when returning from adventures wild,
He saw it rise again o'er ocean's brink.

Steadfast, serene, immovable, the same,
Year after year, through all the silent night
Burns on forevermore that quenchless flame,
Shines on that inextinguishable light!

It sees the ocean to its bosom clasp
The rocks and sea-sand with the kiss of peace
It sees the wild winds lift it in their grasp,
And hold it up, and shake it like a fleece.

The startled waves leap over it; the storm
Smites it with all the scourges of the rain,
And steadily against its solid form
press the great shoulders of the hurricane.

The sea-bird wheeling round it, with the din
of wings and winds and solitary cries,
Blinded and maddened by the light within,
Dashes himself against the glare, and dies.

A new Prometheus, chained upon the rock,
Still grasping in his hand the fire of Jove,
it does not hear the cry, nor heed the shock,
But hails the mariner with words of love.

"Sail on!" it says: "sail on, ye stately ships!
And with your floating bridge the ocean span;
Be mine to guard this light from all eclipse.
Be yours to bring man nearer unto man."

The sweeping vistas of Portland Head Lighthouse are some of the most dramatic on the Maine coast.

Historian Edward Rowe Snow wrote of Portland Head Lighthouse, "Portland Head and its light seem to symbolize the state of Maine—rocky coast, breaking waves, sparkling water and clear, pure sea air."

The stunning Victorian two-family keeper's house was built in 1891, replacing an earlier structure. The house adds to the picturesque nature of the location. The lighthouse was electrified in 1929. During World War II, the lighthouse was dark for three years, and in 1958 the original Fresnel lens was replaced with aero beacons. A storm in 1972 wreaked havoc on the lighthouse. A twenty-five-foot wave broke a window in the keeper's house, washing in mud, aquatic plants and even starfish. The steel fence that surrounded the property was torn asunder and ripped from its concrete foundation. In 1992, the lighthouse was automated and no longer required a lighthouse keeper. Shortly thereafter, a gift shop and museum opened to the public. Today the light from Portland Head Lighthouse can be seen twenty-five miles out to sea.

There have not been many breathtaking moments like the ones I experienced doing nighttime tours at Portland Head Lighthouse. Fort Williams Park is completely dark at night, and when there is no moon out it is like walking into a dark curtain with a shining light on the other side. As you stand at the base of the lighthouse, watching the overhead sweeping beam of the aero beacons as they touch land and sweep out to Casco Bay is a humbling experience. The lighthouse tower almost seems taller at night and the colorful lights from Portland twinkle in the distance above the horizon. Looking out over the bay, beacons from other lighthouses communicate with their flashing lights, each offering their guidance and warning. The silence of this space at night is broken only by the waves crashing against the rocky coast that surrounds the lighthouse. On one night in particular, the waves were over ten feet tall and the ocean splashed over the fences that surround the lighthouse. Off in the distance fireworks blazed over the city of Portland as the *Queen Mary II* came into port. The stories of the lighthouse being haunted seem to blend seamlessly into the dramatic seaside setting.

Some people have relayed stories claiming that when they are in the basement of the keeper's house, another presence is with them. An unseen spirit has caused people to feel that perhaps the spirit of a lighthouse keeper past may be lingering behind. Another persistent ghost story is about the spirit of a little boy who has been seen around the lighthouse. Some people have claimed to see him around the lantern room looking out over Casco Bay. Another spectral character has been seen on the grounds of Fort Williams Park, often heading toward the lighthouse. This character has been described as a man wearing a dark uniform, similar to that which a lighthouse keeper would wear.

Should you visit the lighthouse gift shop, you may come across two unusual images that were taken inside the lighthouse tower. These ghostly photos depict a spectral man and woman who appear to be light keepers of old still attending to their duties. The images were designed and photographed by Michael Francis Barry, who can often be found at the lighthouse selling his dramatic prints. More than two hundred years after it was built, Portland Head Lighthouse attracts photographers, poets, painters and spirits of the past.

The Witches of Falmouth

According to Horace P. Beck in his 1957 book *The Folklore of Maine*, witches can be clearly identified with a few simple questions. Beck suggested that most witches were women, usually unmarried, who liked to live alone. He raised questions for those who may have already been suspicious of a woman who had long, stringy hair, piercing eyes, a thin nose and long, sharp fingers with nails overgrowing their skin. He claimed that their complexions were pale and their voices were high-pitched and raspy. Other identifying traits were that candles would burn blue in a witch's presence, she could make furniture fly around the room and she had powers of transformation and could change into an animal. Other giveaway mannerisms included the inability to cry, bleed or say the Lord's Prayer. The book goes on to say that witches were more often found on the mainland than on the islands, because it was harder to live apart on a small island with a large population. Beck did, however, go on to say that sometimes a witch would move to an isolated island and live alone, but the person would be termed mad or suspected of some dark crime.

During the eighteenth century there were wild superstitions about witches. Some people during that time believed that you could ward off witches with a hex apple. The superstition behind the hex apple was that if you shaped an apple into the image of a human face and hung it in the kitchen over the hearth, it would dry out and ward off any witches. Another superstition practiced at the time was to carry a dried clove of garlic or a sprig of mistletoe to ward off any evil spell. Some who thought that they were the victim of a witch's evildoings would wait until a full moon and then toss dried apple seeds over their shoulder, thereby releasing the curse. As unusual as these customs sound, the stories of witches in Falmouth during this time had odd similarities, whereby just a strange occurrence would cause people to act in a peculiar way.

There is a legend of two witches in Falmouth that dates back to the hurricane of July 31, 1767. One witch was said to be the first to move into a part of Falmouth that became known as Hurricane, because of the severe devastation after the July storm. According to legend, the witch was known as Old Kate and she lived on the old road where the lumber camps used to exist. It was said that the villagers avoided traveling down the old lumber road for fear that Old Kate would put a spell on them and they would never return. On the rare occasion that she came into town, people would look away as she passed by. Some folks feared her piercing eyes, for they believed that the witch could cast a spell with a simple glance.

Another witch who also lived in Hurricane went by the name of Sally Tripp. Whenever something went wrong in the town, the community blamed Sally. It was rumored that Sally could simply touch a plant and that would ruin the crops for the season. One outrageous story came from a man by the name of James Woodsum, who blamed his arthritis on a curse that Sally had carried out against him. He claimed that Sally turned him into a horse every night and rode him up and down what was known as Hurricane Hill. As Sally rode the horse, she would continually whip him and he claimed that was why his body became so twisted. Part of the witch folklore of the day was that witches could easily transform into animals, so no one would suspect them of their craft.

Sally was blamed for other unexplained occurrences of the times as well. Nicholas Hall, who owned a farm in Hurricane, claimed that Sally had cursed him as well. He tried to churn butter one day and he found that it was taking an extraordinary amount of time. He said it was because Sally the witch was in the cream. He claimed that he was going to pound the churn as if Sally's head was in it, and he was going to pound her head off. He churned as hard as he could, with every intention that he was pounding Sally. Just as the cream turned to butter there was a knock at the door and someone said that old Sally Tripp was dying and her head was all swelled up.

After Sally died, she was buried near her small home adjacent to a farm owned by Fred Stuart. The story goes on to say that some years later, Fred Stuart was digging on his farm when he unearthed the remains of a human skeleton. It was described as the skeleton of a small woman who died a very violent death, as was evidenced by a look at the back of the skull, which was crushed in. Further, there were only four teeth, and they were all black in color; Fred thought she must have been a smoker. He knew that Sally was a smoker. The skeleton was allegedly found where Sally Tripp was buried. Nicholas Hall's butter churn was said to be passed down from generation to generation after the discovery of the witch's skeleton was made.

Nearly one hundred years before the witches of Hurricane, there was a sad occurrence that connects Portland to the Salem witchcraft hysteria of 1692. Renowned Reverend George Burroughs preached in Salem, Massachusetts, for a number of years. The reverend was held in high regard wherever he went. At some point during those years, he came to live at Casco (Falmouth). Reverend Burroughs preached at an area known as Black Point throughout 1686. Back in Salem during the witchcraft delusion, the reverend was accused of being a witch because of his large size and great strength, which many believed was representative of supernatural powers. Burroughs also had the misfortune of having his first two wives die. People testified against Burroughs, stating that he was cruel to his wives. It was further said that the two wives visited some of the villagers as visions to inform them that Burroughs had killed them and that he was indeed working for the devil.

Reverend Burroughs was brought from Maine back to Massachusetts to stand trial at Salem. The reverend was found guilty and condemned to death. All the while he proclaimed his innocence through speeches and prayer. On August 9, 1692, he was hanged, along with several others who were also convicted of witchcraft. Reverend Cotton Mather stated that all those who were hanged had died by a "Righteous sentence." This was a tragic end for someone who was wrongly persecuted based on opinions and prejudices.

Approximately thirty years before the unfortunate end of Reverend George Burroughs, there was another unjust witchcraft accusation that took place on Richmond's Island in 1659. A drunken preacher by the name of Thorpe had boarded at the home of Goodman Bailey. Mr. Bailey's wife was so disturbed by the drunken behavior of Mr. Thorpe—which she found to be contrary to his calling—that she told him to reform his life or leave her home. Mr. Thorpe angrily left the Baileys' home and became their enemy. Soon, he seized an opportunity to retaliate against Mrs. Bailey. On the same day Goody Bailey traveled from the island to Casco on the mainland, a cow owned by Mr. Jordan of Spurwink had died. Mr. Thorpe claimed the cow had died of a witch's spell and told Mr. Jordan's servants to put the carcass in the place of his choosing. When the carcass was burned, the witch who cast the spell would show up. The cow was cleverly put on the path that led from Black Point to Casco and was set ablaze. People were amazed when Mrs. Bailey came walking up the path, and Mr. Thorpe had her questioned as a witch.

Fortunately, Mr. Jordan was not predisposed to supernatural explanations. He was a man of common sense, and he rose to Mrs. Bailey's defense. He knew the poor beast had died due to his servants' neglect, and to cover their misdeed they were willing to let an innocent woman stand accused of witchcraft. Because of Mr. Jordan's rational thinking, he saw through Mr. Thorpe's scheme and saved Goody Bailey from standing trial and facing the gallows.

very gold butter
shown curtain-

The Pool Hall Ghost

An article in the August 31, 1991 issue of the *Portland Press Herald* alleges a pool hall poltergeist. Port Billiards, located on 39 Forest Avenue, seemed to be drawing quite a bit of attention, supposedly because of a ghost. The owner, Lee Edwards, felt that the location was haunted ever since the business opened up there in December of 1990. Unexplained late night noises seemed to plague the business during closing time, after all of the patrons had left for the night. Lights were said to turn off and on, and strange incidences convinced the owner that something unusual was going on.

Edwards described that five employees of the billiard parlor had all experienced ghostly activity. Some employees felt that while they were working, there was a presence in the room that couldn't be seen. It was pretty common in the parlor for employees to claim that they felt someone standing behind them, then to turn around and find no one. On one occasion a pool cue thumped against the wall and then flew off the rack and toward an employee who was working the register. Items in the pool hall regularly went missing and would turn up days later.

The incidents have been linked to a murder that happened in the space upstairs from Port Billiards. Back in 1979, when Pine Tree Billiards operated upstairs, there was a robbery and murder of a pool player who was a regular customer. The person who committed the crime confessed and is currently serving time in the Maine State Prison. Edwards believed that the spirit of the murdered man inhabits the pool hall.

When the police responded to a burglar alarm on August 13, 1991, Lee insisted that it must have been the ghost who was playing a prank and

This modern building is the location of the Pool Hall Ghost.

pulled the alarm. The police weren't as convinced and responded with a twenty-five-dollar fine. Other residents in the building were also a bit skeptical about the ghost story, as they claimed they hadn't experienced anything unusual.

A few months later during a Halloween party, everyone was hoping that the ghostly spirit would make some sort of appearance at the billiard parlor. While there were many visible ghosts and specters there that night, some felt the presence of the unseen entity. A few years later, Port Billiards closed, and the building is currently for sale. When the building is sold, will the ghost reappear to the new tenants? Only time—and maybe a burglar alarm—will tell.

The Ghost Bride, Lydia Carver

One of the most tragically romantic tales in Maine is that of the ghost bride, Lydia Carver. Lydia was one of seven children of Amos Carver, who had become a wealthy Portland businessman. Her family had moved to nearby Freeport from the Plymouth area in Massachusetts, and they found success there at the turn of the nineteenth century. Unfortunately, not many personal details are known about Lydia herself, or about the man she was supposed to marry. But what was certain is that her sad tale began in July 1807.

An excited twenty-three-year-old Lydia Carver, along with twenty-one other people (mostly her bridal party), had boarded the schooner *Charles* and set out to Boston, Massachusetts, to have her wedding gown fitted. The captain of the ship was Jacob Adams of Portland, who had brought along his wife, which some of the superstitious passengers thought was bad luck.

On Sunday, July 12, 1807, the schooner sailed off from Boston to complete the overnight trip back to Portland. It was said to be a bright and sunny summer day as the *Charles* made good time on the return journey. As the schooner approached Richmond's Island just before midnight, a severe gale seemed to blow in out of nowhere, and tragedy seemed imminent. The Atlantic Ocean reacted violently, and the waves overcame the *Charles*. The swells caused the schooner to strike Watt's Ledge, just fifty feet offshore from Richmond's Island. The schooner tipped over onto its side, and the bottom of the *Charles* was ripped out.

The passengers on the *Charles* faced their doom in the cold ocean waters as the waves washed over the wrecked schooner. Some of the passengers attempted to cling to the masts and rigging; however, they were no match for the furious sea. Captain Adams and three other men attempted in vain to reach the shore of Richmond's Island. Frantic cries from Adams's wife called him back to the ship, and as he attempted to return to her the waves carried him to a watery grave.

Those who tried to find a way to hold onto the remains of the schooner were forced into the sea, as during the late night hours the *Charles* broke apart. When the storm passed and the morning sun appeared, a devastating scene revealed itself from nearby Crescent Beach. The body of Lydia Carver had washed ashore, and next to her was her trunk holding her never-to-be-worn bridal gown. In all, sixteen people perished that fateful July night. The bodies of the captain and his wife were also recovered, and he was buried in Portland's Eastern Cemetery. Lydia's body was buried in a little countryside burial ground just above Crescent Beach, a short distance from the island.

I first learned about the Inn by the Sea, where Lydia Carver is buried, when I received a call from Rauni Kew, a longtime employee of the inn. Rauni had told me the fascinating story of Lydia Carver, and she invited me up to tour the property and to meet their award-winning gardener, who also had a few tales to share. When I first arrived, I found the inn to be gorgeous and, although I was expecting a small, quaint and cozy inn, I found the property to be more like a luxurious resort. The view of the Atlantic across the salt marsh was most scenic, and the area was teeming with beautiful birds. It seemed to be quite a peaceful setting, a place where you could easily expect a lonely soul to wander. After a brief walk down the pathway, Richmond's Island came into view. It really did seem so close to the mainland. It was easy to imagine the morning after the fateful 1807 storm and envision the schooner's masts twisting above the shoals of the island; what a staggering sight it must have been.

At the end of the walkway was the small burial ground, and after brushing past a bush of fragrant beach roses I found myself standing under a beautiful shady tree at the entrance to the graveyard. Across the graveyard were no more than twenty markers. Some were just fieldstones, while there were a few ornately carved stones dating from the nineteenth century. A tall slate stone in the cemetery appeared to be in flawless condition, almost as if it was placed there just yesterday, rather than in 1807. This was the stone for Lydia Carver, and it appeared to be meticulously maintained. The carving was crisp, and the stone didn't seem to be weathered one bit. The epitaph that briefly tells the tragic tale on the stone was perfectly readable. In fact, the footstone was still standing and also appeared to be in excellent shape. It was rather strange that some of the other stones in the cemetery were not as old, yet they were in much worse condition. Some were barely legible. I was told that Lydia cares for her stone, and that she's been seen in the cemetery near her grave. Perhaps in a sense she is making sure that no one forgets her story as it is told on her stone.

The Inn by the Sea opened in 1982, although stories of Lydia's presence go back much further. Because of the amount of traffic associated with the inn as far as guests, visitors and employees, there are now more stories of Lydia's presence than ever. One of the enthralling stories about Lydia that predates the inn was told to me by an older woman who was a longtime member of the Cape Elizabeth Historical Society. She had stated that in the late 1960s her daughter caught a glimpse of Lydia along Route 77. There are lush meadows and forested areas along this very scenic and quiet road that leads past the Inn by the Sea. I was told that one night as the young woman was traveling the road in her car, she noticed two figures standing along the roadside. As the woman approached, she discovered a lady wearing a long, white wedding gown standing silently resting her hand on a female deer that stood completely still at her side. The woman in the gown made eye contact with the traveler on Route 77, and then as the car passed she vanished; a look into the rearview mirror revealed that there was no one there. The woman's daughter was absolutely certain that she had seen Lydia Carver that night.

More recent stories include tales from the desk clerks, who often see the elevator doors opening into the lobby with no one aboard, although the buttons have been pushed. Late at night when guests are asleep it seems as though there is a phantom joy riding in the elevator. One might think that a ghost might not have use for an elevator—couldn't they just pass through walls?—but perhaps this is a way that Lydia makes her presence known in a playful and visible manner. One of the stories that was relayed to me by a young man on the housekeeping staff was that one morning while cleaning one of the recently vacated suites, he had an encounter with Lydia. He said that he was just finishing up his work when he looked into the bathroom mirror and saw a woman wearing a wedding gown pass by. As he turned to scan the room for anyone else, he found that he was alone, except maybe for the spirit of the ghost bride. He told me that there is a sighting of Lydia almost every week, either from the staff or the guests.

In the late 1980s there was a surprising story about a visitor from Boston, Mark Hardee, and his wife, who were enjoying a relaxing stay at the inn. During their visit they decided to enjoy the views and take a walk along Crescent Beach during the night of July 12 (the same date as the wreck of the *Charles*), and according to his story a most unusual thing happened. Mark arrived at the beach first, taking the half-hour walk along the footpath from the inn. As he made his way along the shore he heard a loud crack, splintering wood and the booming of what sounded like a shipwreck. Following these ominous sounds was a woman's scream that pierced the night from across the water. Listening, Mark also heard other screams from far away that sounded like men, women and children. The men were shouting; the women and children were screaming and crying in terror. Mark strained to see what was happening off in the distance. Mist rolled across the water, and a shadowy silhouette of a ship appeared to be near the dimness of Richmond's Island.

Mark shouted to his wife, as he was uncertain about what was unfolding around him. His wife ran up to his side, the sounds stopped and the apparition disappeared. Mark and his wife quickly made their way back to the inn and recounted their experience to staff members, who found it to be almost too much of a coincidence that the name of Mark's wife was Lydia Carver Hardee. Mark had not known the story of the ghost bride until the staff relayed it to him that night, although after that encounter, he probably hasn't forgotten it to this day.

Lydia has been known to move dishes and place settings around in the dining room in the evenings, for when the staff comes in to prepare breakfast they find the dishes have been stacked up and things aren't as they remembered. Lights have been known to go back on in some rooms at the inn, although people are certain they've turned them off. Many guests have commented that they've felt a presence in their room. One person even claimed to see an indentation in the bed as if someone had been sitting there.

Many people have been attracted to the inn over the years. The band Icarus Witch stayed at the inn, and they found the story of Lydia Carver so compelling that they decided to write a song about the fateful shipwreck of 1807 on their 2005 album, "Capture the Magic." In the credits of the album it reads, "Lydia Carter (R.I.P.) at The Inn By The Sea, Portland, Maine." An excerpt from the song reads as follows:

The view of the Inn by the Sea from Crescent Beach.

"The Ghost of Xavier Holmes"

In the vessel's log a dying man had written;
"I've lost my captain & crew to a darkened and watery grave...
I'm so alone, trying to stay alive"
...What should have been a routine trip has cost the lives of sixteen

The inn is a popular place for weddings on the Maine coast, and all summer long there are parties and celebrations. Many stories about Lydia also come from brides who have unusual dreams, such as their wedding dress floating about their room or mysteriously moving from where it had been hung, with no explanation.

In February of 2007, I had the opportunity to investigate the inn and grounds with a paranormal group from Dracut, Massachusetts, called the New England Ghost Project. Their mission was to see if they could connect with the spirit of Lydia Carver. The investigation was accompanied by the local newspapers and approximately fifty tour guests, all hoping for a glimpse of the ghost bride. Almost immediately during the investigation, the psychic medium Maureen Wood said, "Lydia is here." Maureen began to channel the spirit of Lydia, and she said that her spirit was sad and blamed herself for the loss of the other passengers aboard the *Charles*. Apparently the thought in Lydia's mind was that if it wasn't for her wedding, none of the people would have been aboard the schooner, and they wouldn't have perished. Lydia also wanted to communicate that she enjoyed being at the inn and around all of the many brides-to-be, as she was never able to be a bride herself. It was quite amazing to see Maureen crying as she responded to the questions that were being directed to Lydia. The entire group stood in silence during the experience. However, just as soon as Lydia's presence was with the group, within a few minutes she had moved away…only to be discovered down the hall in one of the suites, where the group headed next.

In the beautiful townhouse-style suite where the ghost project had some of their equipment stored, the group's organizer, Ron Kolek, was missing his EMF (electromagnetic field) reader. He was certain he had it in his bag when the group arrived. Maureen attempted to make contact with Lydia through dowsing. Dowsing, or rhabdomancy, is believed to date back over six thousand years and was used by the ancient Egyptians and Chinese. One of the uses of dowsing is to make contact with the paranormal world by helping to provide yes/no answers to questions. In response to Maureen's questions, it appeared that Lydia made her presence known again, and just moments later she was gone. Before the group left the room, Ron checked for his EMF reader again in his bag, and he found it. He was certain that he had checked the bag thoroughly before, and it had most certainly not been there. Yet after the presence of Lydia in the room, the meter mysteriously reappeared.

On the second floor of the inn toward the end of the hallway where the suites are, there is a framed black-and-white engraving that seemed to draw the attention of the ghost project. The image was of a woman's body that had washed ashore, her hand still clinging to a rope, as she was cradled by a fisherman. Off in the background were an island and a ship that had wrecked on the island. The masts were broken and splintered. There were over a dozen engravings along the hall, but none displayed a scene like this one. As medium Maureen stood next to this particular illustration, she felt as though Lydia was present again, perhaps in her own way indicating that this image displayed her sad fate.

As the group made their way onto the grounds of the inn for the next part of the investigation, the restaurant host came up to me and said that

Where did this mysterious portrait of Lydia Carver come from?

there was a psychic from Boston having dinner that night in the Audubon Room. The psychic was very interested in what the group was doing and asked if she could join in. The group stepped out into the wintry gardens with another curious psychic. As everyone prepared for the outdoor portion of the experience, tour guests started to take their cameras out for the chance to perhaps capture a spirit's image. It was then that several people started commenting that their cameras were not working. Even though their cameras had just received new batteries at the beginning of the evening, eight people had their camera batteries completely drained of power, which left many people on the tour puzzled. While people were fidgeting with their cameras or digging for fresh batteries, both psychics said that Lydia was present again.

Along the walkway the group walked, toward the small cemetery where Lydia was buried. But before the group got to the white picket fence that borders the burial grounds, someone in the group exclaimed that he just got a digital image of an orb floating above the group. At that moment everyone began taking pictures in several directions and one after another you could hear people say, "I've got one," and, "Look, here's another." Even a newspaper reporter pulled me aside to verify that she captured the image of an orb. One of the orb images shot above the graveyard was quite interesting, as the orb revealed a ring-like structure, and it appeared to be moving through the air in a series of circles. Even those who seemed a little bit skeptical were very surprised at some of the images they captured on that tour. Our investigation was truly a fascinating and "spirited" experience.

On the third floor of the inn is a lovely dining area, and just around the corner is a lovely portrait of a young woman in a satin wedding gown, who the management of the inn believes is Lydia Carver. Although it is most peculiar that there is no one in the inn who can verify where the painting came from, it has been hanging on the wall for years. The sweet expression of this woman, assumed to be Lydia, makes her tragic story even more touching.

A visit to the Inn by the Sea will yield beautiful views, an elegant property, a peaceful cemetery and beautiful gardens. Employees at the inn state that they truly enjoy Lydia's presence, and that they have grown quite fond of her. Although travelers and joyous bridal parties visit the inn for a brief time, Lydia the ghost bride is always there, a sweet, lost soul who may wander this place eternally.

The Casco Bay Sea Serpent

Sightings of strange sea creatures have surfaced in many newspaper articles about Casco Bay over the years. During June and July of 1818, a "long beast" was reported in the waters not far from Portland Head Lighthouse. The captain of the vessel was certain that he had seen this beast raise its head out of the water at least thirty to fifty feet. The ghastly creature was seen heading in the direction of the lighthouse.

An account by Ole Mikkelsen of Portland stated that he encountered the creature in June 1958. Mikkelsen was born and raised in Denmark and had come to Maine in 1923. Accompanied by another man, Mikkelsen woke up early that summer morning to go fishing in the waters off Cape Elizabeth, about one and a quarter miles south of the Portland Lightship. He described seeing what he thought was a submarine, but upon a closer look he discovered that he was seeing a live creature. The tail of the creature surfaced over the water, and the serpent dove under the water several times. Mikkelsen's reporting went on to say that the creature appeared to be well over one hundred feet long, and it turned to look at the two men in the boat. As quickly as the creature had appeared, it turned away from Mikkelsen and his companion and headed southeast through the mists. Mikkelsen thought that the creature was attracted to the sounds of the Portland Lightship's horn. Watching the creature in Casco Bay Harbor for forty-five minutes, both men were certain that they had encountered a sea serpent.

There is a house in the Western Promenade of Portland that has a curious iron gate. Along the top of the gate are two sea serpents twisting their tails near two battle-axes. Perhaps the residents of this stately house have their own story about the Casco Bay sea serpent.

The gate to this historic home in the Western Promenade hints at further sea serpent tales.

The Victoria Mansion

One of the most magnificent places I have visited in Portland is the Victoria Mansion. I lost count of how many times I said "wow" out loud during my tour. Located at 109 Danforth Street, the Morse-Libby Mansion was built as a summer home for Ruggles Sylvester Morse, a Maine native who made his fortune in the hotel trade in New Orleans. This magnificent home was built in the Italian villa style and is said to be one of the most significant historic house museums in the country. Since Morse had an extensive background in luxury hotels, he certainly would have a home that was just as luxurious. The mansion was built between 1858 and 1860, just prior to the Civil War. The contrast between the light and shadow of the shapes in the façade is remarkable, and the structure warrants close examination of every detail. A handsome brownstone exterior features a four-story tower and a beautiful front porch and entranceway.

When Ruggles Morse passed away in 1893, his widow sold the house to Joseph Ralph Libby, who was the founder of a popular Portland department store on Congress Street. The Libby family lived in the house for over thirty years. The family then moved out in 1928, and dark days drew near for the mansion. In 1940, the mansion was about to be scheduled for demolition, but luckily someone recognized the home's significance. A retired educator, William H. Holmes, was able to purchase the property and establish the house as a museum in 1941, named for Britain's Queen Victoria. In 1943, Holmes transferred ownership of the mansion to the Victoria Society of Maine, which has held stewardship over the house ever since. The efforts of the society are evident throughout the mansion, and their goal is to preserve and interpret this magnificent place for future generations.

Is the Victoria Mansion haunted by a musical ghost?

If the outside of the mansion seems impressive, the interior is extraordinary and spectacular. Morse sought out the best designers and architects of the time. It is said that the mansion is the only Herter commission that exists in the country. More than 90 percent of the interior is original, including furniture from the Herter workshops, magnificent gasoliers, stunning stained glass and sophisticated ceiling and wall murals.

The enormous flying staircase in the entryway is an architectural marvel. The outdoor light filters through the stained-glass ceiling, which features cherubs representing each of the four seasons. While most of the stained glass in the mansion is original, some of it had to be replaced due to a hurricane, but the replacements blend seamlessly with the original pieces. The myriad of dazzling colors create a rainbow of lights along the staircase and walls.

So many rooms of the mansion have their own stories to tell, and each is most inviting, as well as a feast for the eye. The gothic library on the first floor is fascinating. The room appears to be taken from a sixteenth-century castle. The walls of hand-carved wooden bookshelves still hold an enormous collection of books. The chair behind the desk is carved with the initials R.M. for Ruggles Morse, and you would almost expect him to breeze past you and have a seat. The nearby dining room features a porcelain luncheon and dinner service that was made in France and was used by the Morse family. The ceiling in the dining room is a bit of an illusion, as it looks like a variety of carved wood placed in an elaborate design. Upon closer inspection you will find that the illusion is created by a painted mural. Giuseppe Guidicini, an Italian immigrant who lived in New York City, was commissioned by Morse to do all of the mural work throughout the mansion. The realistic style of painting not only created the perfect illusion of wood, but also the likeness of plaster carvings in other areas of the mansion. Also on the first floor there is a painting of a mansion that looks quite similar to the Victoria Mansion. This painting used to hang in Buckingham Palace and was donated to the mansion because of the resemblance.

The theme of the first-floor living room is love. In the chandelier there are cherubs with bows and arrows pointing down at unsuspecting visitors. The enormous paintings in this room also resonate the theme of angels and love. Taking a closer look at the sitting chairs in the room, you will find carved cherubs in the arms. However, the feet of the chairs are cloven hooves. The tour guide explains that the Morses said that while the room represented love, it also showed the dark side. Therein lies the good and evil dichotomy that could easily be overlooked in this room.

On the second floor of the mansion are two bedrooms, a music room and a most unusual room, the likes of which I had never even heard of before. Hidden behind glass doors is a Turkish smoking room. This incredible private room features a comfortable couch and decorative chairs. The colors are a combination of rich reds and purples, and the room is accented with numerous tassels. The gasolier in this room was designed to be pulled down so that the smokers could use it to light their cigars or whatever else they were smoking. An investigation into the smoking materials is planned to be conducted over the next few years when the wallpaper in the room is chemically analyzed. The Turkish smoking room is said to be the first documented room of its kind in a private home.

In one of the bedrooms is a lovely portrait of a little girl holding flowers and dressed in a beautiful gown. But the painting requires closer inspection. In the background of the image are dying plants, and the area around the girl's head is completely black. The painting is said to be of Morse's niece, as the Morse family never had children of their own. The

The elaborate architecture of the Victoria Mansion is a standout of the nineteenth century.

painting was a death portrait that was painted right after the little girl died. This practice was common during Victorian times, as many families either had photographs of their deceased children taken or portraits commissioned.

The remainder of the rooms on the second floor are filled with more wonders and beautiful period antiques. On the third floor of the mansion is a large billiard parlor, designed to entertain guests. I believe that a house this elaborate with rooms that have such character certainly must have some ghost stories. The tour guide alluded to the fact that he wanted to stay overnight in the mansion to see if the place "was really haunted." That statement prompted the question, "What makes you think it's haunted?" Reluctantly, the tour guide told me a ghostly tale from the mansion. On the second floor in the music room is a beautiful piano that is original to the mansion. The tour guide explained that sometimes as he is bringing tours in the room throughout the day, he will notice that the pages have been turned in the book. Sometimes a new book has been placed on the piano, but all of the books are kept securely in a case in the room. The furnishings and piano in the room are behind a barricade that no one crosses, not even the tour guides. So what is the explanation for the mysterious music books? Maybe the spirits still enjoy a little piano music in between shifts of visitors to this glorious mansion.

Halfway Rock Lighthouse

Halfway Rock Lighthouse stands on a barren three-acre rocky ledge in the middle of Casco Bay. Looking across the horizon from Portland Head Lighthouse, you can see the tower of Halfway Rock Lighthouse. Dangerous shoals and ledges surround the lighthouse, and its purpose is to warn mariners to steer clear. In 1835, the ship *Samuel* ran aground on the rock due to the fact that the ledge is only ten feet above sea level on a clear day. The ledge easily becomes submerged during storms, and the rock has been underwater as much as eight feet during storms; that's when it becomes perilous. The construction of the stone tower took nearly one year, and finally construction was completed in 1871. In 1888, a boathouse was carefully constructed on the island. The light keepers lived inside the lighthouse tower on different floors, in very close quarters, as the boathouse was only used for boats and storage. After nearly eighty years, the original boathouse was replaced, and finally a new keeper's house was built along with a helicopter pad. However, in 1972, a severe storm washed away the buildings, and all that remains today is the lighthouse tower. The red signal can be seen for twenty nautical miles out to sea.

There was an occasion during the 1960s when two lighthouse keepers were attempting to land on Halfway Rock for their stay at the light station. The ocean waves proved quite challenging for the men as they tried to land their boat, and a wave washed the men's television out of the boat and into Casco Bay. With the loss of their only source of entertainment at the light, the men were forced to play an unusual game. Each man kept score of how many flies he killed in the lighthouse tower; the one with the most fly kills was declared the winner.

George A. Toothaker served as an assistant keeper and later head keeper at Halfway Rock for twelve years, from 1872 to 1885. The lighthouse seemed to exude a presence that affected Keeper Toothaker. Years after the keeper ended his assignment on the island, he described his experience at the light. The former keeper even claimed that being at the light station drove one man insane. Being a lighthouse keeper at an isolated station like Halfway Rock certainly took a special kind of person. It was a lonely and desolate life. In the winter and during storms the island was inaccessible. There was no vegetation on the island, nothing grew and there wasn't even a place to take a walk on this tiny pile of rocks. Lighthouse keepers were often superstitious, and they followed strange customs to make sure that they survived their time at the light. Some keepers wouldn't whistle in the tower, for they thought that whistling mocked the devil and it would cause him to summon up his satanic powers and create a fierce gale. Another superstition related to carrying buckets of water. Keepers would make sure that the buckets were full to the top with water, for even the slightest bit of space left open would cause evil spirits to enter the bucket and enter the lighthouse. There were even thoughts that the sea was controlled by spirits, and some keepers would not sail on Fridays, because Friday was supposedly the day of the devil.

Keeper Toothaker was interviewed by a local newspaper, and he claimed that even though it had been years since he had been at Halfway Rock Lighthouse, he was still haunted by the light. He said that he would often wake up out of a sleep to feel the darkness on the island surrounding him, as if the light in the tower had gone out. He claimed that the night hours left him unsettled and any strange sounds would bring him back to the days of being at the lighthouse, fearful that the light was about to go out.

Today the lighthouse at Halfway Rock is automated, and there are no longer any keepers on the island. Instead, there are solar panels on the tiny island that power the light. It is interesting to ponder the story of Keeper Toothaker, who was haunted by the lighthouse long after he had left Halfway Rock.

The Blaidsell House

The Blaidsell House is an attractive seaside residence on Cape Elizabeth that has an unusual ghostly tale associated with it. This large home was the subject of an unknown phenomenon in 1793. The story tells of an apparition of a woman who appeared to the Blaidsell family. The apparition made an odd request of the Blaidsell family: she said that she was looking for her father, Dr. David Hopper.

Captain Paul Blaidsell and his wife Lydia sent a message to Dr. Hopper, and he arrived, not certain what to expect. Hopper allegedly questioned the spirit, attempting to confirm her identity. Questions that related to the family history were put to the spirit, and Dr. Hopper confirmed it was the spirit of his deceased daughter. The word of the haunting quickly spread throughout town, and everyone began to show up at the Blaidsell home to experience the ghostly spirit. The story further goes that Reverend Abraham Cummings thought the story was a fraud and he decided to unmask this deception. When the reverend arrived at the house, much to his surprise he witnessed a rock levitate and transform into a mass of bright, white light. Subsequently the mass of light changed into an apparition in the shape of a woman. The community began to recognize the spirit of the doctor's daughter, as she appeared with a blinding white light around her. The story went on to say that upward of fifty people gathered in the cellar of the Blaidsells' house to hear the phantom speak. The ghostly specter was said to pass right through the bodies of the amazed crowd. According to the legend, the spirit had messages that she wanted to communicate, including the importance of proper moral behavior. Before the spirit left that evening, the locals said that she also accurately foretold the death of the homeowner's wife and father.

Portland's Mystery Tunnels

What lurks beneath your feet as you walk the streets of Portland's downtown areas conjures up a variety of images. It seems as though there is always a mysterious attraction to what we may not see, but yet may be so very close to us. Tunnel configurations under busy seaport cities are not uncommon. There is a famous tunnel system under the port of Seattle, Washington, where in fact visitors can go and tour the labyrinth in what appears to be an underground city. Portsmouth, New Hampshire, also has an extensive tunnel system that is still being discovered under old buildings and busy public streets. There are numerous reasons for tunnels, such as the Underground Railroad, the connected network of safe houses that helped slaves escape to freedom during the Civil War. Local legend speaks of a tunnel that connects the historic Tate House to the Stroudwater River that was used for the freedom efforts.

Another use for tunnels was for shanghaiing, when unsuspecting people were passed through a network of secret rooms only to discover themselves onboard a ship when they awoke. These captives were forced to work on their ship in order to pay back a debt that they owed to the captain. Typically the captain of a ship would secretly pay off the debt of a person, and in turn that person would unwillingly be made a sailor. With the high amount of maritime trade and shipbuilding in Portland, would it be such a stretch to say that this was possible?

Some of the rumors about Portland's tunnels include a tunnel in the Old Port section of town. Certainly it would not have been unusual to have tunnels that connected the numerous warehouses and factories along the waterfront during the late nineteenth and early twentieth centuries. It was common at that time to move goods from place to place by using wheeled carts through a system of tunnels underneath warehouses. It is said that one of the buildings on Exchange Street still exhibits archways in its architecture, and allegedly these archways were part of a series of passageways that led from the waterfront up toward city hall.

There were also rumors of tunnels beneath busy Congress Street. In the early twentieth century, Congress Street was compared to bustling streets in New York's downtown. No matter where people seemed to be going, they all passed through Congress Street. The new city hall that opened in 1912 and the city's first skyscraper, the Fidelity Trust Building, were just part of this busy complex of buildings. A number of department stores opened up that brought women and homemakers to Portland. Numerous theaters with their brightly colored posters and busy window displays also added to the appeal of Congress Street. A tunnel of seemingly endless passageways was rumored to zigzag its way underneath the street. Reportedly a tunnel system originated underneath the Eastland Hotel, which was built in 1925 and was the largest hotel north of New York at the time. It is said that passageways led from under the hotel to Forest Avenue and High Street.

There were also stories of tunnels that were built underneath Fort Gorges, perhaps connecting the fort to the mainland or other islands in the bay. Construction on Fort Gorges began in 1858 and was completed in 1865. Originally the fort had an armament of ninety-five guns. This fort is quite noticeable from several points in Portland and South Portland. It is topped with greenery from the numerous trees and shrubs that grow there. A closer view of the fort can be obtained on the Casco Bay Lines Ferry as it passes by the fort on its regular route to and from the islands. Direct access to the island can be gained by private boat only. Some locals claimed to have obtained access to the tunnels on the island in the 1950s and 1960s. One story from a resident on nearby House Island states that a man went exploring the tunnels at Fort Gorges and never returned. Does the ferry sail along the same route as the mysterious tunnel? Perhaps, but no one seems to know for certain.

In 1996, *Casco Bay Weekly* reporter Elizabeth Peavey investigated the mysteries of Portland's subterranean depths, and that article states that "she lived to tell the tale." Elizabeth explored the basements of many buildings, as she was guided by business owners who stated that there was nothing to discover. Persistence led Elizabeth to continue to ask questions of the historical society and the library, but while everyone she spoke to had heard rumors of the tunnels, none of them could confirm their existence. Throughout Elizabeth's research she never seemed daunted by the dead ends she kept experiencing. For every instance that a tunnel wasn't revealed, another story about a tunnel's existence came to light. In summary, Elizabeth said that she wasn't ready to dismiss the existence of tunnels, and that perhaps there was also a network of people in town who were keeping some secrets shrouded in darkness, much like the legendary tunnels.

The International Cryptozoology Museum

Portland, Maine, may seem like an unlikely place to find the International Cryptozoology Museum. Loren Coleman is a Portland resident who is working on making his dream a reality. Coleman describes cryptozoology as the study of hidden or unknown animals. He has been tracking down reports, accounts, sightings and other evidence to determine if there is any credible information that may further knowledge about a "cryptid" (an unknown or mystery animal). Since March of 1960, Coleman has spent his days traveling the world, interviewing "witnesses" and writing books on the subject.

In August 2003, Coleman took his retirement savings and opened the museum in a house he purchased in Portland. The museum features a collection that he obtained through researchers, scholars, colleagues and the general public. Included in the museum are Hollywood cryptid-related props such as *The Mothman Prophecies*' Point Pleasant "police" outfit. There are an eight-foot-tall life-size Bigfoot model and plaster foot casts of the Yeti and Bigfoot in the collection. A saber-toothed tiger skull, special art and sculpture creations by some of the leading cryptozoological artists in the world are also featured. If you've ever wondered about the existence of Sasquatch, this museum may hold the answers. Coleman is accepting donations of mysterious animal items to the museum, and he hopes that his collection will aid in the understanding and investigation of these legendary creatures. These undiscovered creatures are not only on land, but also in the ocean: Coleman has been known to investigate strange fish and lake monsters. Loren Coleman is an experienced scientist and takes his work very seriously in hopes that his discoveries will lead to answers. The growing museum is open by private appointment, and hopefully soon the museum will be open to the public on a regular basis. Who knows what strange creatures lurk in the dark woods of Maine—Loren Coleman does.

Beckett's Castle

Beckett's Castle is located in Cape Elizabeth on a private road that leads to the ocean. The gothic stone castle is complete with a three-story tower that has a shadow of mystery over it. Sylvester Beckett had the castle constructed in 1871. The castle is accented by sharp peaks and large picture windows. A successful Portland attorney, publisher and poet, Beckett often wrote about the things in life that fascinated him the most. In the poem "Hester, the Bride of the Islands," Beckett offered his thoughts on death:

> *Life, spirit, soul! They come and go*
> *But whence or whither who can say*
> *A something dwells within, we know*
> *And finds expression through the clay*
> *If the soul dieth, if our years*
> *On earth, of discord, joys, and tears,*
> *Be all of life, then life is vain,*
> *And Heaven's great work imperfect!*
> *No! Death is but a second birth—*
> *And man, immortal, oft returns.*
> *Such things are not illusions—Nay*
> *Nay still do man-immortals sway*
> *In life's affairs! And often blend*
> *With souls of earth in sweet commune.*

Beckett strongly believed in the afterlife and often held séances in his home, and he frequently invited a few select friends to join him. Beckett's circle of friends consisted of local artists, journalists and philosophizers.

To prove that there was life after death, Beckett swore that his spirit would return from the dead. In 1882, coinciding with Beckett's death, strange occurrences began happening in the castle. New owners reported seeing a blue form shaped like a human change into a strange mist that moved throughout the castle. Strange knocking sounds occurred on the door to the castle tower, and often an unexpected cold breeze whooshed past when the tower door was open. Some people wondered if the cold breeze could have been a draft, while others insisted that it was Beckett's spirit, as he had spent much time in the tower taking in the views of Casco Bay.

One resident said that she often found the pictures and photographs that were hung on the walls moved from place to place. Perhaps Sylvester Beckett preferred his own arrangement and moved the pictures to suit his own tastes. Other unusual phenomena included bedsheets being pulled off of beds and found in piles on the floor. A door in the castle opened so often on its own that the owner decided to nail it shut, but the door kept opening, pulling the nails right out of the wall.

The castle changed hands a few times over the years, and in the 1980s the owner was so certain of the ghostly presence that she called in a psychic to confirm her thoughts. Another séance was held at the castle, but this time it was Beckett who was the subject of contact. The psychic believed the house was still inhabited by Sylvester Beckett, at least in spirit form. The owner was happy that she could have someone confirm what her senses and experiences were. A few years later the castle was sold again, and the current owners haven't discussed the ghostly history, nor do they wish to have unexpected curiosity seekers.

One can only wonder whether Sylvester Beckett's spirit still inhabits the castle to prove that there is life after death, or if he hasn't left the property simply because he still enjoys the view from his tower.

Twin Lighthouses of Cape Elizabeth

There are not too many places left in the United States where there are still twin lighthouses standing. The Twin Lights of Cape Elizabeth are just another reminder of Casco Bay's maritime history. These two lighthouses stood witness to many important moments in the area's seafaring history. At one point the early lighthouses were distinguished by unusual "daymarks." These daymarks served to visually separate the lighthouses for sailors at sea. The west tower was painted with one broad, vertical red stripe and the east tower was painted with four horizontal bands of red.

The current lighthouse towers, built in 1874, stand at sixty-seven feet tall and are three hundred yards apart. As thick walls of fog regularly blew in along the coast, a loud fog signal was needed, and a signal house was built a short distance from the light keeper's house. This building contained a ten-inch locomotive whistle that blasted every minute for eight seconds when fog when present. To distinguish the lighthouse station from others on the coast, one light was fixed while the other one flashed so that mariners could tell they were approaching Portland Harbor.

A severe storm blew in during the winter of 1885 and is chronicled in one of the most dramatic pages in the lighthouse's history. The lighthouse keeper, Marcus Hanna, was quite ill when his wife woke him one morning to describe a frightening scene on the ledge near the lighthouse. The vessel *Australia* tried to keep the course from Boothbay to Boston; however, the storm raged violently against all the seamen's efforts. A fierce wave struck the vessel and washed the captain into the frozen waters of Casco Bay. Keeper Hanna waded into the frigid ocean and attempted to rescue the two remaining sailors who clung to the broken rigging. Even though

The east tower and keeper's house of the Twin Lighthouses of Cape Elizabeth.

the lighthouse keeper was feeling very ill, he managed to save each of the sailors in one of the most dramatic rescues in United States lighthouse history. Keeper Marcus Hanna later received a gold medal of valor for his amazing rescue.

In 1924 the government decided to change all twin light stations to single lights, and the light at the west tower was permanently extinguished. Just one year later the light at the east tower was increased, making it the second most powerful lighthouse in New England. Today the light can be seen fifteen miles out to sea. In 1934, lighthouse Keeper Joseph H. Upton, at the age of sixty-five, went to light the auxiliary light because the light in the lighthouse had failed. At 11:30 p.m. that night, Keeper Upton's wife wondered about her husband's absence, and when she went to the lighthouse she made a heartbreaking discovery. At the bottom of the spiral staircase the unconscious body of Keeper Upton was discovered; he had fallen down the staircase and fractured his skull. The keeper was brought to the hospital, where he died a brief time later. Upton had experienced a long life of being a lighthouse keeper, as he had also served at White Island Lighthouse in New Hampshire and at the twin lights of Matinicus Rock, twenty-five miles offshore from Rockland, Maine.

During World War II, the lantern room was removed from the west lighthouse and the tower was converted into an observation post. Also during World War II, the keeper of the east tower was ordered to extinguish the light during a coastal blackout. The keeper also owned a small cottage in the area that he rented to a woman who often complained about the light from the lighthouse waking her up during the night. After receiving orders to turn out the light, the keeper stopped by the woman's cottage to tell her that he had turned off the light so she could sleep. The woman picked up the newspaper the next day and found out that the keeper had been joking.

In 1971, the west tower was purchased by actor Gary Merill (Bette Davis's ex-husband), and many of the locals thought that Gary was quite an eccentric. The community was astonished to see Gary make his way through town with his donkey, riding in the back of his Cadillac convertible. The west tower changed hands a few more times during the following years.

Today the keeper's house next to the east tower is privately owned, and the property is off limits to the public. However, many people have said that on the grounds of the lighthouse an older man wearing a lighthouse keeper's uniform has been seen disappearing near the tower. Some people claim to have seen this mysterious spirit standing at the bottom of the driveway to the keeper's house. It has been suggested that the spirit is that of Keeper Joseph Upton, who perished back in 1934. Perhaps the spirit of the lighthouse keeper is still keeping watch over the bluffs by this beautiful lighthouse.

The McLellan-Sweat House

S ome say the history of Portland's Federal architecture *is* the grand McLellan-Sweat House at the junction of High and Spring Streets. A striking and yet dignified Federal mansion, the house has been called the finest example of its type in northern New England. This stunning mansion was constructed in 1800 and in 1972 it was designated as a National Historic Landmark. The painted tan brick and brilliant cream-colored trim add to the air of elegance this notable home retains. The shade of a neighboring ancient copper beech tree creates shadows of long branches and moving leaves as the wind blows up the hill past the house. Welcoming visitors to the front door is a semicircular English columned portico and exquisite Palladian window. Surrounding the house is an attractive fence accented with twenty-two-foot-tall urn-shaped finials, also painted to match the cream-colored trim on the house.

The McLellans were prominent and successful shipbuilders, and Major Hugh McLellan was president of Portland's first bank. However, the family lost their fortune just a short time after having the house built. The Embargo Act of 1807, which was a prelude to the War of 1812, struck a fatal blow to the wealth and success of the McLellan family. The mansion was sold to the bank in order for Major McLellan to pay off his debts. The mansion was then purchased by Colonel and Mrs. Lorenzo Sweat in 1880. Upon Mrs. Sweat's death in 1908, the house, along with a sizable endowment, was given to the Portland Society for Art. Until 1911, the house served as Portland's only museum and art school, and a gallery was dedicated to the memory of Colonel Sweat. For many years in the late 1980s, the museum remained closed, and dust and drop cloths seemed

The stunning McLellan-Sweat House is a visual masterpiece.

to be all that was on display. Throughout the 1990s, dedicated efforts were put forth to make necessary repairs to the mansion and restore the structure to its original grandeur. The efforts of those involved are evident just by standing outside of the house. Today the house is open to the public as part of the Portland Museum of Art, inviting visitors to take a peek inside this stunning home and visit the world-class gallery. While today the museum houses priceless artwork and sculpture, the house itself is a most spectacular piece of artwork.

Alex Tanous is a noted psychic and teacher of parapsychology at the University of Southern Maine, and during a visit to the historic home he immediately felt the presence of spirits. There was a cold, phantom breeze when Tanous stood at the bottom of the stairs, as he contemplated the existence of spirits in the fascinating home. Nineteenth-century music, as if from a grand party, was heard by Tanous, and yet there was no source for the sound. Spirits swirled around Tanous as he made his way through the house, as if there were partygoers moving from room to room. It is said that Mrs. Sweat often had grand parties and celebrations that drew hundreds of people to the home. The history of the house

Do spirits of the past still linger at the McLellan-Sweat House?

was so compelling, Tanous thought, that there was some sort of psychic impression left behind. Energy from the spirits seemed to glow from within the house, much like the fantastic chandeliers may have been glowing during celebrations.

A visit to the McLellan-Sweat House will provide the visitor with an education in fine art and sculpture. A walk through the peaceful courtyard adjacent to the High Street entrance presents a carefully tended pocket garden with beautiful, fragrant flowers. However, standing in the shadow of this amazing house provides the backdrop for the stories of spirited partygoers who in their own way still celebrate the past and present of this grand mansion.

The Ghost of the 1868 Victorian House

An article in the *Portland Press Herald* stated that Evelyn Ross was probing ghostly activity in her 1868 Victorian home. The presence of the female spirit was so strong that often she would be seen sitting and rocking in the chair in the home. The ghost was also said to be musical, as the owner of the house often heard singing and the strumming of what sounded like a mandolin. At other times the spirit would make herself known with the sounds of banging on the walls and television. The owner described one unnerving incident when she answered the phone late one night, and there was a mysterious caller on the other end of the line. The voice coming through the phone was described as not completely human, having an odd metallic sound. When Ross hung up the phone, she noticed that the phone was not connected to the wall.

Pictures that hung on the wall of the antique home mysteriously flew across the room without explanation and personal items disappeared and reappeared in other rooms of the house. Ross wasn't the only one to experience this active spirit; visiting friends also reported seeing the ghost in the house. On one occasion the owner's five-year-old granddaughter claimed to have seen the ghost. Finally, late one night Ross was awoken by someone sitting down at the end of her bed. The female presence appeared to be looking over the owner while she slept. While some people met Ross's encounters with skepticism, she was very convinced that something odd was happening in her home.

With all of this unexplained activity, the owner decided to call in a psychic investigator. When the psychic arrived at the house, she stated that she could sense the spirit. The psychic decided to communicate with the ghost in a channeling session, where she could ask questions of the spirit. Immediately during the session, the psychic felt that the spirit was a friendly entity who was caught between the earthly world and the spirit world. The spirit had not crossed over upon her death, but her mission was to protect Ross. In fact, the psychic relayed that the ghost had saved Ross's life in a recent car accident. After the psychic had reassured Ross about the spirit's presence, she felt that her house wasn't necessarily "haunted." Ross decided that the ghost was more of an unseen roommate, and she was happy to have her company.

The Pirate Ghost Ship

The famous privateer ship the *Dash* was built at the beginning of the War of 1812 in Portland by the Porter brothers, who were prominent merchants. The ship was outfitted at private expense for the purpose of preying on enemy commerce to the profit of the owner. Shipbuilders of the eighteenth and nineteenth centuries took great pride in their work, and many ships like the *Dash* often took on a bit of personality. A lot of thought and some superstition went into the building of ships, in hopes of assuring a prosperous future. The keel of a ship was often constructed on a favorable day, but never on Fridays. The greatest care was taken to be sure that no one was hurt or killed during the building, for that could tarnish the fortunes of the ship. Ships were never painted blue for fear that the great ocean spirit would be jealous. In addition, the name of the ship was carefully selected, making sure it didn't sound too humble or too haughty so the sea spirits would not be offended. One of the traditions also intended to seal good fortunes when a ship was launched was to have a minister read a prayer and knock three times on the hull to drive out witches that may have secreted themselves inside the depths of the ship.

The profits from privateering were quite lucrative, and the business attracted recruits from all walks of life, including politicians, lawyers, blacksmiths, grocers and ministers. In most cases every occupation in the city was represented in the ownership. Further, this ownership did not involve just one person alone, but often was a share purchased by the entire family. It was said at one time that there were nearly thirty privateer ships sailing from Portland. The *Dash* became famous when a young twenty-four-year-old captain named John Porter (a younger brother of the ship's owners) took the helm. The *Dash* was living up to its name, as it was thought to be one of the fastest ships of its time in Portland.

During January of 1815, Captain Porter seemed ready for another adventure, and he made way for what would soon be the last known voyage of the *Dash*. But something that night warned Captain Porter—if only he had heeded the sign. While bidding his newlywed wife a fond farewell, he heard a warning gun on the ship go off; however, he still lingered behind with his wife. During his departure from her home, he hesitated once again, and upon hearing the second warning shot he waved his final goodbye and boarded the eager ship.

When the *Dash* set sail it met a newly launched privateer ship from Portsmouth, New Hampshire, in Portland Harbor. The visiting ship was ready to challenge the *Dash* to a race of speed. The ships passed the lighthouse at Portland Head and by the end of the next day the *Dash* was in the lead, following a southerly course. All of a sudden a severe gale blew in and the ship from Portsmouth changed its course and headed back toward Casco Bay. But what of the *Dash*? It was thought that the *Dash* fell victim to the storm and was never seen again. Some versions of the story remark that there was an ominous omen that followed the ship. Some locals believed that blue birds were seen following the ship when it left the docks in Portland, which was a sign of a tempest striking within forty-eight hours. Mysterious tempest or not, none of the crew was ever found, and no wreckage ever washed ashore.

When news reached Portland, the relatives of the lost loved ones vowed never to give up hope. As locals made regular climbs to the top of the Portland Observatory, a silent vigil was kept for the beloved crew and ship. Despite their hopes, the ship and its crew were lost forever.

It was said that the family of the captain's bride did their best to comfort her when she heard the storm blowing in on that fateful night. Upon mentioning the name of the ship, something fell in the parlor. A tile from the fireplace had fallen off upon the uttering of the words the *Dash*, and some thought that incident was an omen that the ship had been lost.

Many stories have come from local sailors over the years about the doomed ship. The ship had been seen sailing the waters of the bay with tattered sails that couldn't possibly hold the slightest of breezes. There was also said to be a phantom crew that stood on deck and stared straight ahead. The crew was described as skeletal spirits with weatherworn expressions. Whenever the ship was approached, it would disappear. Some said that seeing the ship foretold of death, and some sailors who saw it were so frightened that they thought just seeing the ship was a curse.

One story tells of an incident in August 1942 when the U.S. Navy and Her Majesty's Navy patrolled the waters of Portland during World War II. A wailing siren resonated across Casco Bay as the HMS *Moidore* swept into the bay. A local man named Homer Grimm, who had been enjoying the afternoon on one of the Casco Bay Islands, later relayed the incident from his vantage point. He said he saw a tall ship sweeping past the island, tearing through the waves. He described seeing sailors on the deck straining to see into the approaching mists. In the distance, Homer saw the HMS *Moidore*, the U.S. Navy and the Coast Guard all with guns rattling and sirens wailing in pursuit of the elusive ship. Straining to see the name on the mystery ship, Homer finally caught the name on the stern: it was the *Dash*! The *Dash* disappeared into the mists and when the Allied forces passed the island where Homer Grimm was, the phantom ship was nowhere to be found.

In an eerie nineteenth-century poem written by poet John Greenleaf Whittier, the legends of the infamous privateer ship the *Dash* were immortalized in verse.

"The Dead Ship of Harpswell"
By John Greenleaf Whittier

What flecks the outer gray beyond,
The sundown's golden trail?
The white flash of a sea-bird's wing,
Or gleam of slanting sail?
Let young eyes watch from Neck and Point,
And sea-worn elders pray,—
The ghost of what was once a ship
Is sailing up the bay!

From gray sea-fog, from icy drift,
From peril and from pain,
The home-bound fisher greets thy lights,
O hundred-harbored Maine!
But many a keel shall seaward turn,
And many a sail outstand,
When, tall and white, the Dead Ship looms
Against the dusk of land.

From Pirates to Ghost Brides

She rounds the headland's bristling pines;
She threads the isle-set bay;
No spur of breeze can speed her on,
Nor ebb of tide delay.
Old men still walk the Isle of Orr
Who tell her date and name,
Old shipwrights sit in Freeport yards
Who hewed her oaken frame.

What weary doom of baffled quest,
Thou sad sea-ghost, is thine?
What make thee in the haunts of home
A wonder and a sign?

No foot is on thy silent deck,
Upon they helm no hand;
No ripple hath the soundless wind
That smites thee from the land!

For never comes the ship to port
Howe'er the breeze may be;
Just when she nears the waiting shore
She drifts again to sea.
No tack or sail, nor turn of helm,
Nor sheer of veering side;
Stern-fore she drives to sea and night
Against the wind and tide.

In vain o'er Harpswell Neck the star
Of evening guides her in;
In vain for her the lamps are lit
Within thy tower, Seguin!
In vain the harbor-boat shall hail,
In vain the pilot call;
No hand shall reef her spectral sail,
Or let her anchor fall.

Shake, brown old wives, with dreary joy,
Your gray-head hints of ill;

And, over sick-beds whispering low,
Your prophecies fulfil.
Some home amid yon birchen trees
Shall drape its door with woe;
And slowly where the Dead Ship sails,
The burial boat shall row!

From Wolf Neck and from Flying Point,
From island and from main,
From sheltered cove and tided creek,
Shall glide the funeral train.
The dead-boat with the bearers four,
The mourners at her stern—
And one shall go the silent way
Who shall no more return!

And men shall sigh, and women weep,
Whose dear ones pale and pine,
And sadly over sunset seas
Await the ghostly sign.
They know not that its sails are filled
By pity's tender breath,
Nor see the Angel at the helm
Who steers the Ship of Death!

Legends of the Casco Bay Islands

The Casco Bay Islands are romantic, mysterious and are steeped in legends and lore. Native peoples called the bay Auccocisco, meaning "the place of the heron." The Native American presence is recorded in the shell mounds found on the shores of many of the islands. The Casco Bay Islands were originally named the Calendar Islands by explorer Captain John Smith in the seventeenth century, as he thought that there was an island for every day of the year. Today it is said that there are about 220 "official" islands in Casco Bay. The unmatched beauty and peaceful ways of these islands have their own special appeal. While not all of the islands can be visited by the casual sightseer, there are some that are open for hiking and quiet exploration. Ferries from Portland are the best way to begin exploration of the islands. It has been said that there have been upward of fifty shipwrecks along the islands in Casco Bay. The *Edward J. Lawrence* burned at the docks of Portland Harbor in December of 1925, and a fireboat and tugboat attempted to drag the burning wreck out to sea. When the fire burned down to the shackles holding the anchors, the *Edward J. Lawrence* fell to the bottom of the sea between Diamond Island and Fort Gorges. The unique view of Portland and the Maine coast from these islands is unforgettable, as are the ghosts and spectral stories that surround them.

Cliff Island

Cliff Island is a gorgeous island with approximately seventy-five year-round residents. This quiet island is accented by sweeping ledges that overlook the Atlantic. There are a variety of nineteenth-century summer cottages on the island as well. One of the island's claims to fame is that it was the location of the movie *The Whales of August*, which was filmed in 1986 starring Bette Davis.

Cliff Island has the fascinating tale of a hermit who was a reputed "mooncusser." The origins of the name "mooncusser" are quite interesting. It is said that because the moon's rays mirror and enhance the water's surface, sailors could see very well on moonlit nights, even when the moon was only partially full. Therefore, decoy lanterns would not fool experienced mariners under these circumstances. As such, when the mooncussers' deceptions did not succeed, they often shouted, "Cuss the moon!" into the moonlit night. Captain Keiff was thought to be a smuggler and a pirate, and he lived all alone on this island. During storms, Keiff would fasten a lantern to his horse's neck and ride back and forth across a narrow stretch of the island in hopes that he would lure passing vessels to their doom on the treacherous reefs. Ships that were hoping for shelter from the storms became wrecked on the island with no escape. Oftentimes the crew would fall victim to the combination of the perilous shoals and the unrelenting weather.

Captain Keiff would make sure that there were no survivors and he would bury the bodies of the unfortunate sailors on a grassy knoll near a deep ravine. This area has come to be known as Keiff's Garden. Keiff would then salvage the ship's cargo and any valuables he could find, making for a very unique way of life. After his mission was complete, he would returned to his log hut to await the next storm.

Jewell Island

Jewell Island is composed of about 221 acres and lies on the outer edge of Casco Bay. It was named after George Jewell, who was the island's first occupant in 1636. A wonderful fishing port, the main harbor is called Cocktail Cove, so named for the pleasure boaters who still gather there for merrymaking in the summer months. One of the many stories about the island is of a small schooner that wrecked in 1846, and all six men onboard perished. The bodies were recovered and buried on the island in an area that was marked with fieldstones. The graveyard was eventually forgotten and blended in with the landscape of the island. It is rumored that the burial ground lies somewhere near the center of the island.

Throughout the island there are ruins of the military installation that was built when the island was seized for the defense of Portland Harbor during World War II. The remains of these abandoned structures add to the fascination of the island. There is also a fifty-foot observation tower on the island that was constructed during the World War II occupation, which affords visitors grand views of the islands and Portland Harbor. Caves and underground tunnels are also part of the extensive complex of buildings. Some people have claimed to hear mysterious voices coming from within the empty tunnels.

The island also holds a great legend that concerns a pirate from Bermuda and buried treasure. It is said that the pirate and his crew buried their entire ship in an area on the southern end of the island known as Punch Bowl Cove. Years later, the pirate and his crew returned to the spot and excavated the ship and its cargo of treasure.

Another tale from the islands features the well-known and notorious pirate Captain Kidd. William Kidd was born in Scotland around 1645, and although his affair with the sea began early in his life, there isn't much known about him until 1689. Kidd's career as a pirate sent him all over the world, and he amassed quite a treasure over the years, including everything from gold bars to the finest jewels. A bounty was placed on Captain Kidd's head, and he was forced northward from the Caribbean Islands. The story goes on to say that he found his way to Falmouth Harbor, where he made a plan to bury his treasure.

Legend tells us that Captain Kidd was attracted to Jewell Island because of its sheltered cove. The island must have seemed the perfect place to bury his treasure. He took a large copper kettle from the ship's galley and filled it with his best plunder. Kidd then sent most of the crew to an inland spring to fill water buckets while he buried the treasure, so that the whereabouts would be a secret. Captain Kidd commanded the remaining crew to dig a hole for the treasure, and when it was buried he had them cover the spot with a large flat rock.

Before Captain Kidd departed the island, he carved an inverted compass on the rock, pointing south instead of north. Captain Kidd was later convicted of the murder of William Moore and was sentenced to hang by the House of Commons in London, England. On May 23, 1701, Kidd was taken to the feared execution docks to meet his fate. The first time he was strung up, the hangman's rope broke and he had to be hanged a second time. After he was cut down it is said that he was laid in the tides to let the sea wash over him three times. He was then painted in tar, bound in chains and put in a metal harness that kept his skeleton unbroken as his flesh rotted away, a practice that is known as gibbeting. His body was then hanged at a point where it could be seen by those sailing in or out of the Thames River, as a warning to would-be pirates. Although he was pressured before his death to reveal where his treasures were buried, Kidd only revealed a few locations, and most of his fortune was never recovered.

Bailey Island

Bailey Island was originally called Newaggin, a Native American name for the place frequented in spring by a branch of the Abenakis known as the Nequssets. Europeans began settling the area in the 1730s and 1740s. The island is named for the first resident, Timothy Bailey, a parish deacon who built a garrison to protect colonists from the Indians. Bailey Island feels very much like a world apart, and Land's End on the island is the farthest out into Casco Bay that you can drive directly from the mainland. It is said that during Prohibition in the 1920s, the island was a cache to bootleggers who used the island as a drop off point for wooden cases filled with liquor. Bailey Island is a bit bigger than others in Casco Bay and, unlike most of the others, is accessible by bridge. The bridge that connects to the island is one of the only of its kind in the world: it is a crib-stone design made out of slabs of granite, laid in an open latticework so that the water can pass through. Mackerel Cove is a picturesque spot that invites both professional and amateur photographers with great subjects. A small island, it's just 2.4 miles long, barely half a mile wide at its widest point, with about five hundred year-round residents.

The island was home to a most unusual resident, known as the Acaraza Man, who said he could make silver coins from morning dew. He in fact formed a corporation for that purpose in 1801. Interestingly enough, the business failed, but not before he collected fees from several naive investors and then fled with their money.

Pirates were said to have frequented the island, including at least one who left a kettle of gold coins hidden in a hole by what are known today as the Cedar Ledges. It's said that during the nineteenth century, treasure seekers would dig on the beach seeking riches they had only heard about. Some stories tell of men who would hear a clunking sound as they dug deeper into the ground, perhaps indicating that there was a chest buried there. Hours and days of digging would go by, and what sounded like the possibility of treasure turned out to be nothing. Some locals say perhaps the spirits made sure that the treasure would never be found. However, in 1840, gold coins were discovered by a man who sold them in Boston, Massachusetts, for $15,000, according to the *Casco Bay Breeze*, a local newspaper. Maybe the spirits decided to finally allow the treasure to be discovered.

Haskell Island

Located just south of Harpswell Neck and west of Bailey's Island, Haskell Island offers up its own unique folklore. The beautiful sheltered cove of the attractive island is an abundant location for fishing. Cove Haskell Island is appropriately named for the two brothers who purchased the island and operated a saltwater farm there. The brothers were said to be both hardworking and successful. It's said that one day a ship came to the island and some rats got loose and proceeded to be an annoyance to the Haskell brothers. The multiplying rats seemed to get into everything, from the supplies to the grain and fish. The brothers figured the best way to control the havoc that was being brought upon them was to bring two cats on the island. While the cats seemed to do the trick of ridding the island of the rats, bigger problems loomed ahead for the brothers. The cats began to multiply and with no natural enemies, they began to take over the island. The cats became bold and hungry, and they raided the catches of fish and slaughtered the hens on the island.

One brother became quite ill and the other went to retrieve him a doctor. Upon his return, he found his ailing brother dead, having been attacked and half eaten by the voracious felines. The surviving brother was said to have destroyed all the remaining descendants of the uncontrollable cats. The brother continued to live on the island and vowed to hate cats until his dying day. According to legend, some old islanders said that there were some cats who escaped being killed and that their descendants are sometimes seen looking down from the treetops on the island.

Great Chebeague Island

Great Chebeague Island has its share of ghost stories, too. There is a little-known woodland path lined with pine trees that leads to a place known as the "Haunted Cellar." The story about the cellar has been passed down from generation to generation on the island. The legend tells of Mrs. George Leonard, who often brought visitors into her kitchen and invited them to sit in what were rumored to be the most comfortable chairs on the island. Mrs. Leonard claimed that the cellar was a real place with a real ghost, and the story had been handed down to her by her mother and grandmother.

The story continues that a house was originally built by the Webber family over an old cellar hole. One night the Webbers heard a tap coming from inside the cellar door, and when they opened the door there was a man standing there in the dim light with blood running down his chest from a gash in his throat. They slammed the door closed. When the Webbers got enough courage to reopen the door, they searched in vain for the ghastly character, but he wasn't there. The cellar had no other door, so how else could the specter have disappeared?

Another islander, Henry Bowen, said that his mother worked in the house above the haunted cellar, and she heard dreadful noises coming from the basement on a regular basis. She described the sounds as someone beating on the side of the house with a club, all along the clapboards.

One tale of the haunted cellar dates back to 1850. A woman known as Granny Hamilton spoke of a story her Great Uncle William Littlefield had told her. She said her uncle saw men carrying chests across his field, not far from the haunted cellar. The men walked the chests down to the harbor toward a little cove near Rose's Point. The mysterious men then loaded the chests into small boats and disappeared around the point. Great Uncle William ran out of his house and traced the men's tracks through the wet morning grass, back across the island and directly to the haunted cellar. The discovery of where the trail went intrigued Great Uncle William, and he decided to round up a group of island men and revisit the cellar. When the men arrived at the haunted cellar, they heard horses galloping wildly in their direction, coming right at them. The thundering sounds of the wild horses grew louder and louder, yet the men never saw a single horse appear.

Another tale spoke of a little girl who attempted to make her way back home across the island when a storm blew in. The girl had to run past the haunted cellar to get home, and as she ran by the cellar she heard the wild horses coming for her. Fearing the horses more than the impending storm, the little girl cried uncontrollably and when she found a nearby house she pounded on the door until someone let her in.

It seemed as though no one could live in the house with the haunted cellar for long, as there were numerous stories about strange things happening to people who attempted to make the place their home. Two families were both living in the house at the same time and each thought that the other family was moving out because of all the loud banging. The sounds that were coming from the house were as loud as if someone was moving furniture and boxes between the rooms. Each family confronted the other, only to find that neither could explain the source of the disturbing sounds.

Next door to the house with the haunted cellar there was a barn that was used to store a hearse. One day a local man was turning hay in the nearby field when he got an ominous feeling from the barn. The farmer said that he heard a loud fluttering coming from the barn, like the sounds of hundreds of birds, and he put down his pitchfork to go and investigate. When the farmer opened the door to the barn, he found nothing more than the black funeral carriage occupying the barn. The door was then closed and the curious man went back to work in the fields, still focusing on the barn as he went about his chores. All of a sudden the sound of hundreds of birds singing came from the barn. The farmer was so startled that he ran home to tell his wife, but he felt that what he experienced coming from the barn was an omen and something bad was going to happen soon. Sure enough, shortly after the farmer's experience, Nicey Ann Littlefield Long gave birth to her first baby, and Nicey died. The funeral carriage in the barn next to the haunted cellar was used in the ceremonies. Nathaniel Long, Nicey's husband, was so distraught over her death that he was seen standing on Rose's Point, the point of land that he owned, where he made the decision to leave the island. Soon after leaving the island, Nathaniel Long was lost at sea. Some of the locals say that before Nathaniel left the island he had buried some of his money on Rose's Point.

Eventually the house that was above the haunted cellar was moved away, but even with the house gone the stories persisted. It is said that a man who claimed to be a descendant of the original family that lived in the house went to the cellar to see if he could dig up whatever treasure had been buried there. The islanders watched the man, and he soon became irritated by the crowd's presence. While digging one day, the man was accosted by one of the islanders, who jumped into the cellar hole with him. The would-be treasure hunter told the islander that he would be cursed and that he would die a sudden and violent death within a year, and they would have to break his back to put his body in a coffin. Everyone on the island was certain at this point that the man digging had gone completely mad. But within a year the man who jumped in the hole became deathly ill with typhoid, and he died during a convulsion, all doubled up. In order to fit the dead man into the coffin, his back had to be broken.

Conclusion

Portland, Maine, offers visitors a progressive city with a rich heritage and history. From the beautiful views of the Casco Bay Islands to the majesty of Portland Head Lighthouse, locals and visitors alike will find the location simply inspiring. According to the *Guinness Book of World Records*, Portland is the only city in the country with one street on which a person could suit all of his or her educational needs. A preschool, two elementary schools, a middle school, two high schools and a branch of the University of New England are on two-mile-long Stevens Avenue.

Located at 1 Beanpot Circle in Portland, near Route 295, is the B&M Baked Bean factory. The building was originally occupied as a canning facility up until the Civil War. There is even a bit of lore associated with baked beans. It is said that the Pilgrims wouldn't cook on the Sabbath, so the women made pots of baked beans and kept them on the fire through Sunday. The B&M Company is known around the world for their beans, traditionally made with salt pork and molasses.

Over the years, several popular breweries have had headquarters in Portland, including McGlinchy's and the John Morgan Brewing Co. The city remains famous for its microbreweries, such as Shipyard, Allagash, Sea Dog, Geary's and Gritty McDuff's. This number of breweries stands in stark contrast to the temperate sentiments in the city nearly one hundred years ago, when liquor was outlawed.

Park Street Row is a historic collection of row houses that has evolved over the years. This was the largest row house complex built in Maine. Built in 1835, it was constructed as twenty attached, five-story, seventeen-room, single-family Greek Revival homes of red brick on

This is one of the stunning Victorian twin mansions on Spring Street.

granite foundations. Fourteen of those original buildings survive today. The architectural details of the units survived years of neglect and abuse from the 1950s through the 1970s. However, through the 1980s and 1990s, a renewed interest in this fascinating structure prompted restoration and renovations. One unit even boasts a large nineteenth-century Hope-Jones Organ (the same company designed the organ at Radio City Music Hall, in New York), which occupies a large section of the living room in one of the units. Today this building is one of the most sought-after locations for those looking for a residence with historic appeal.

Historic buildings and contemporary office towers blend with bustling wharves of lobstermen, fishermen and pleasure boaters. Greater Portland Landmarks, an organization concerned with the preservation of the city's historic structures, has designated over nine hundred buildings within the city to be significant. From Victorian charm to modern character and maritime museums to trendy nightclub hot spots, this New England city is worth exploration. Some residents enjoy the area so much that they have both their winter and summer homes in Portland. They spend winter on the mainland and summer on one of the many-storied Casco Bay Islands.

Throughout the many streets in Portland, Maine, there are numerous places that serve as backdrops for tales of ghosts, superstition and mystery. There are certainly more stories that have yet to be told from this old settlement. This amazing city has risen from the ashes time and again, each time with a richer history and perhaps more ghost stories. Every beautiful historic location in the city and along the Casco Bay Islands offers its own unique personality and legacy to passersby. Will you stop and listen to the stories of Portland's ghostly history?

Bibliography

Bec, Horace, and Arthur Healy. *The Folklore of Maine.* Philadelphia, PA: Lippincott Publishers, 1957.

Bruce, Noah. "Who's Buried in Longfellow's Tomb." *Portland Phoenix*, October 26, 2001.

Coleman, Loren. *Mysterious America: The Revised Edition.* New York: Paraview Publishers, 2001.

Costello, Stephen. "Psychic Probes Odd Happenings." *Portland Press Herald*, November 1, 1989, 29.

Englert, Martha. "Pool Hall Poltergeist Reported." *Portland Press Herald*, August 31, 1991, 1, 8A.

"Falmouth Witches." *Portland Sunday Telegram*, October 7, 1934, 7.

Friends of Casco Bay. www.cascobay.org.

Gaines, Judith. *A World Apart. Boston Globe*, July 10, 2005.

Goold, William. *Portland in the Past: With Historical Notes of Old Falmouth.* Bowie, MD: Heritage Books, Inc., 1997.

Greater Portland Graves. www.greaterportlandgraves.com.

Bibliography

Greater Portland Landmarks. *Portland*. Portland: Greater Portland Landmarks, Publishers, 1986.

—————. www.portlandlandmarks.org.

Harrison, Timothy E. *Portland Head Light: A Pictorial Journey Through Time*. Wells, ME: Foghorn Publishing, 2006.

Jones, Herbert G. *Old Portland Town*. Portland: The Machigonne Press, 1938.

Konstam, Angus. *The History of Pirates*. Guilford, CT: The Lyons Press, 2002.

"Legends of Casco Bay." *Portland Press Herald*, July 1, 1972, 112.

Lighthouses of New England, a Virtual Guide. www.lighthouse.cc.

MacPherson, Rick. "Tales From the Boneyard." *Casco Bay Weekly*, October 26, 1995.

New England Curiosities, tours of local legends, lore and mystery. www.newenglandcuriosities.com.

Peavy, Elizbeth. "Stories from Portland's Underground." *Casco Bay Weekly*, January 25, 1996.

Portland Convention and Visitor's Bureau. www.visitportland.com.

"Portlandiana: Casco Bay's Sea Serpent." *Portland Monthly*, May 1986.

Snow, Edward Rowe, with updates by Jeremy D'Entremont. *The Lighthouses of New England*. Beverly, MA: Commonwealth Editions, 2002.

Spirits Alive. Friends of the Eastern Cemetery, Portland, Maine. www.spiritsalive.org.

Bibliography

Stevens, C.J. *The Supernatural Side of Maine*. Phillips, ME: John Wade Publisher, 2002.

Thompson, Courtney. *Maine Lighthouses: A Pictorial Guide*. Mt. Desert, ME: Cat Nap Publications, 1999.

Tree, Christina, and K.W. Oxnard. *Maine, an Explorer's Guide*. Woodstock, VT: Countryman Press, 2003.

Trueworthy, Nance, and Davis A. Tyler. *Maine's Casco Bay Islands, A Guide*. Camden, ME: Down East Books, 2007.

Verde, Thomas. "Alex Tanous, Ghostbuster." *Casco Bay Weekly*, October 27, 1988.

Wallace, Alexander. "The Life of a House." *Greater Portland Magazine*, June–July 1991.

———. "Park Street Row." *Greater Portland Magazine*, December–January 1991–1992.

"Waters of Maine—Mysterious Tales." *Portland Press Herald*, September 26, 1964, 22.